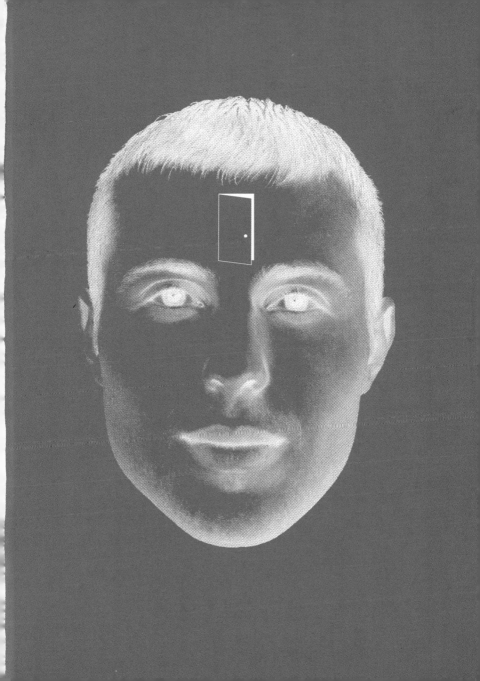

Original concept and Written by Michael Powell
Executive Editor: James Tavendale
Edited by Katherine Robinson and Ewan Carpenter
Illustrated by Allen Boe and AnnDréa Boe
Photography by AnnDréa Boe
Designed by Allen Boe

Metro Books
122 Fifth Avenue
New York, NY 10011

ISBN-13: 978-1-4351-1334-3

Printed and bound in China
3 5 7 9 10 8 6 4 2

MIND GAMES

by Michael Powell

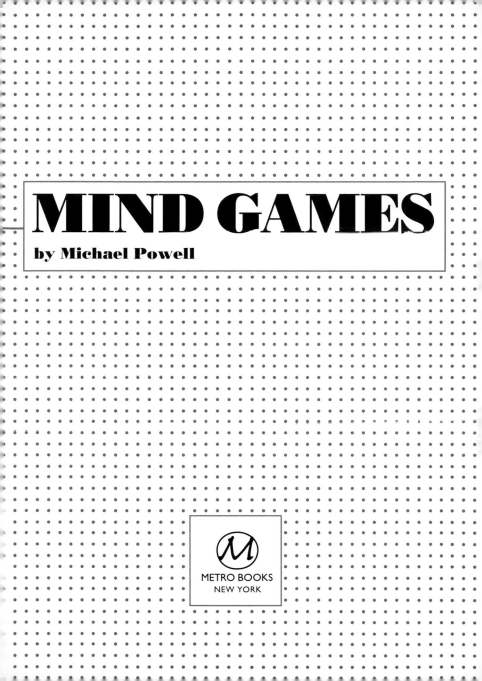

METRO BOOKS
NEW YORK

Introduction

The brain is a three-pound supercomputer with 100 billion nerve cells and more connections than there are stars in the universe. It determines how you think, feel, move, communicate, and stay alive, and yet it's composed of 85 percent water and some fleshy bits.

It's a truly amazing achievement. You should be very proud of your brain because you grew it yourself. And the more you use it, the bigger and heavier it gets! Did you know that if all the neural connections between your brain cells were laid out end to end they would reach to the moon and back?

That said, there's still an ocean of untapped potential in all that gray matter. So why not develop it? Use it rather than lose it! Some of the most extraordinary achievements have been made by people with ordinary brains. They just used them a little differently than other people.

A quarterback wins games not just because of superior technique—but because of his mindset. This book shows 50 ways to unlock some of the mysterious potential in your brain so that you can achieve things you never dreamed possible. Some of them are tricks, some are applied science, and others involve intriguing ways of relearning the way you think. Either way, it's all in the mind.

Table Of Contents

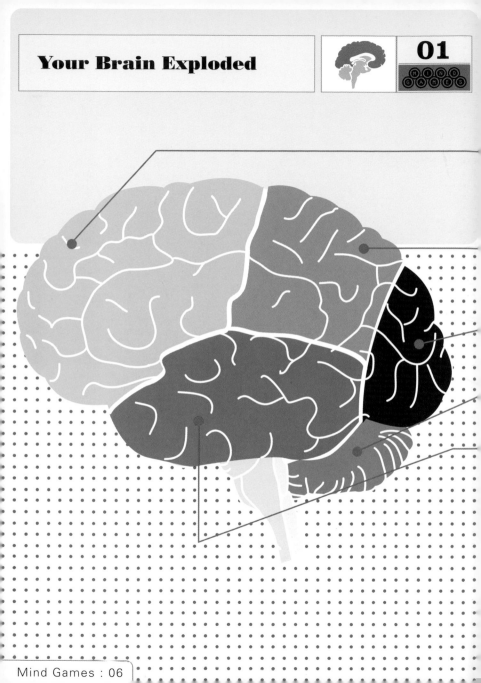

The Cerebrum

Frontal Lobe
Planning, organization, problem-solving, personality, behavior, emotions, conscious thought, speech, memory, motor skills, speech production.

Parietal Lobe
Processing of sensory input, body orientation.

Occipital Lobe
Visual reception and interpretation.

Cerebellum
Coordination of limbs and movements.

Temporal Lobe
Audio and language reception, memory retrieval.

Corpus Callosum
Connects right and left hemispheres.

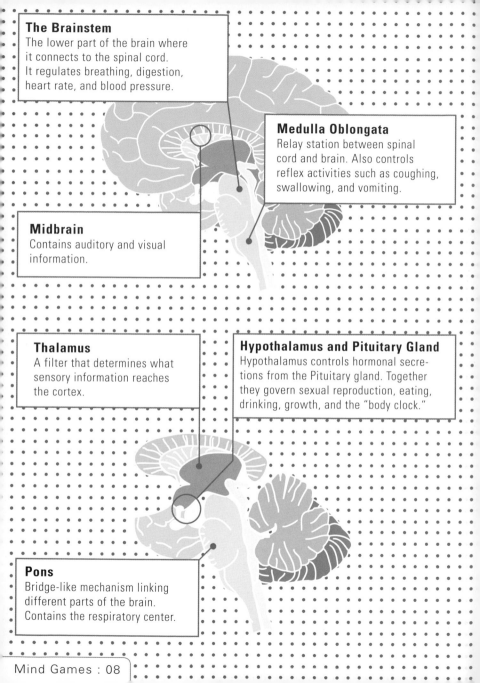

The Brainstem
The lower part of the brain where it connects to the spinal cord. It regulates breathing, digestion, heart rate, and blood pressure.

Medulla Oblongata
Relay station between spinal cord and brain. Also controls reflex activities such as coughing, swallowing, and vomiting.

Midbrain
Contains auditory and visual information.

Thalamus
A filter that determines what sensory information reaches the cortex.

Hypothalamus and Pituitary Gland
Hypothalamus controls hormonal secretions from the Pituitary gland. Together they govern sexual reproduction, eating, drinking, growth, and the "body clock."

Pons
Bridge-like mechanism linking different parts of the brain. Contains the respiratory center.

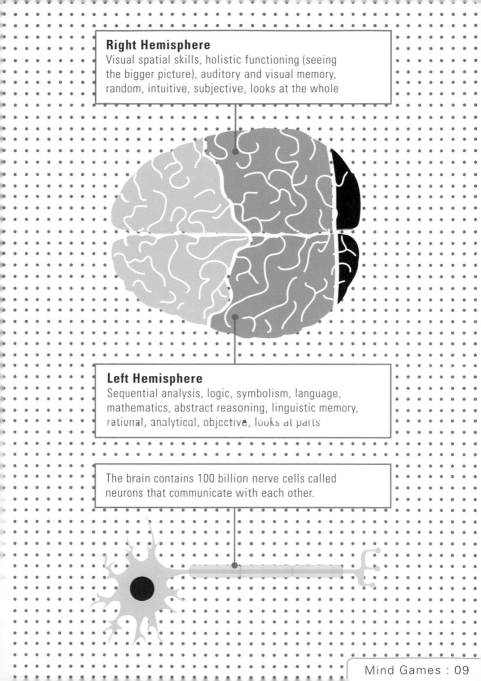

Right Hemisphere
Visual spatial skills, holistic functioning (seeing the bigger picture), auditory and visual memory, random, intuitive, subjective, looks at the whole

Left Hemisphere
Sequential analysis, logic, symbolism, language, mathematics, abstract reasoning, linguistic memory, rational, analytical, objective, looks at parts

The brain contains 100 billion nerve cells called neurons that communicate with each other.

Feed Your Brain

What you eat has a profound effect on how your brain functions. Eating the right food in the correct portions at suitable times will give you mental and physical energy all day long. Here are 10 ways to nourish your brain:

1. Certain vitamins are essential to normal nerve and brain function:

- **B^1** (thiamine) found in whole-grain bread, rice, and pasta
- **B^5** (pantothenic acid) found in meat, poultry, fish, whole-grain cereals, legumes, milk, vegetables, and fruit
- **B^6** (pyridoxine) found in chicken, fish, pork, liver, kidney, whole-grain cereals, nuts, and legumes
- **B^{12}** (cyanocobalamin) found in eggs, meat, fish, poultry, and dairy products
- **C** (ascorbic acid) found in fresh fruit and vegetables
- **Folic acid** found in bananas, orange juice, fortified cereals, leafy vegetables, dried beans, and peas

2. Watch your carbs. Your brain uses up 20 percent of your body's carbohydrate requirements, but it likes them to arrive nice and steady. When your blood sugar levels become erratic, your brain function plummets. Junk and processed foods release sugar into the bloodstream quickly, triggering the release of insulin, which gobbles up the sugar. This sends your blood sugar levels way down low, so your body then has to release carbohydrates from your liver. This yo-yo effect is very bad for your concentration and mood.

3. Brain-friendly carbs have a low glycemic index, which means they release their sugars slowly (which your brain prefers). These include fruit (not fruit juice), whole-grain cereals (not sugar coated) and grains, vegetables (except potatoes and carrots), milk, and yogurt.

4. Graze throughout the day on nutritious foods that are low in fat and sugar.

5. Eat a high-protein meal with complex carbohydrates for breakfast to make you alert.

6. Eat a higher calorie, higher carbohydrate, lower protein meal in the evening to help you sleep.

7. The more simple sugars that are in your meal, the more serotonin your body produces, which is a brain sedative. Therefore if you eat lots of sugary food, you are actually putting your brain to sleep.

8. DHA (docosahexaenoic acid), an omega-3 fatty acid, is a primary structural part of your brain tissue, so make sure you are getting enough. Rich sources of DHA are found in coldwater fish (sardines, tuna, salmon), fish oils, and flaxseed oil.

9. Avoid hydrogenated and partially hydrogenated fats that are high in trans-fatty acids because they impede brain function.

10. Drink at least eight glasses of water each day (see page 12).

Drinking Water

Your brain is your biggest liquid asset. It is composed of more than 85 percent water. Little wonder then that if you are dehydrated, your thinking ability drops dramatically, as does the performance of your whole body.

Deborah Boardly, assistant professor of health promotion and human performance at the University of Ohio in Toledo says, "I truly believe that dehydration may be the number one nutrition problem for athletes—and, possibly, people in general. . . . We have all these concerns about everything we should and shouldn't eat—and yet here is this absolutely fundamental substance and it is grossly overlooked."

Everyone knows how to drink water. You open your mouth, put the glass to your lips, tip, and swallow. This section isn't about how but why you should drink eight glasses of water each day to keep your brain and body in peak condition.

1. Water is second only to oxygen in survival. A body can live for minutes without oxygen, for a few days without water, and several weeks without food.

2. The human body is 60 percent water, blood is 90 percent water, muscles are 75 percent water, and bone is 25 percent water. Water is one of the main structures of the body. Drain your body of water and you'll be left with a few pounds of chemicals that are worth about $5.

3. Your brain is one-fiftieth of your total body weight, but it receives 20 percent of the blood circulation, so one-fifth of your body's water requirements come from your brain.

4. Water balances and regulates almost every other system in the body—temperature regulation, digestion, and waste excretion. You cannot eliminate toxins from your body with insufficient water.

5. Most headaches and feelings of fatigue are caused by dehydration.

6. You lose about 10 cups of fluid each day in sweat, urine, and bowel movements. Even the air you exhale contains vital water vapor.

7. If you wait until you are thirsty to drink, you are already dehydrated. Unlike hunger, thirst is a bad sign.

8. Drinks that contain caffeine (colas and coffee) are diuretics, which means they lessen the body's ability to absorb and retain water—they rob the body of water.

9. It is the most time efficient way of improving your mood and overall performance. It takes seconds to drink a glass of water, but the benefits last for hours.

10. Combined with a healthy diet, drinking water increases weight loss.

"[Polygraph screening] is completely without any theoretical foundation and has absolutely no validity . . . the diagnostic value of this type of testing is no more than that of astrology or tea-leaf reading."

—*former Supervisory Special Agent Dr. Drew C. Richardson, FBI Laboratory Division*

If you reject the lie behind the lie detector test, you have taken your first step towards beating it. It claims to be better than 90 percent accurate, but it has not even been validated through peer-reviewed scientific trials. The truth is, it depends more upon trickery and mind games than science.

"Polygraph" means "many-graph" because it is an instrument that measures your pulse (cardiograph), blood pressure (sphygmograph), the sweat response (galvanograph), and your breathing (pneumograph). Contrary to what happens in movies, the graph pens don't go into overdrive whenever you tell a lie. The operator compares the four physiological response readings to those recorded during certain "control" questions, which set a baseline truth response.

Therefore, if you can display abnormal or heightened responses during the control questioning, the results will be inconclusive, because your baseline readings will be ambiguous. Don't try to hide your feelings by remaining abnormally calm. It is better to do the opposite. When asked a control question like, "Are the lights on?" you should increase your responses by tensing your muscles, doing mental arithmetic, thinking anxious thoughts, or even biting your tongue.

The average polygraph test will usually last two to three hours. The longest part consists of a pretest interview, which may last up to 90 minutes. The test will be explained to you, your legal rights will be defined, and there will be a discussion of the "issue." Many guilty parties give more away at this stage than when they are wired up to the polygraph. The examiner has been trained to manipulate your thoughts and feelings—the polygraph is merely his or her biggest "prop," designed to make you feel vulnerable. The truth is, it is the examiner you must beat, not the machine.

From beginning to end the polygraph process is designed to induce feelings of guilt, even in so-called "honest" subjects. The induction is designed to make you believe in the absolute infallibility of the polygraph test. If you already believed that the polygraph is scientifically valid, you have long ago been duped by the propolygraph propaganda machine that uses Hollywood and the media to make us buy into the lie.

Be aware that some control questions are decoys, and not measured at all. The operator will claim that he or she can spot such deliberate sabotage, but that is another mind trick. The safest bet is to induce panic at every response.

HOW CAN A POLYGRAPH POSSIBLY DETECT TRUE PANIC FROM FAKE? **IT CAN'T.**

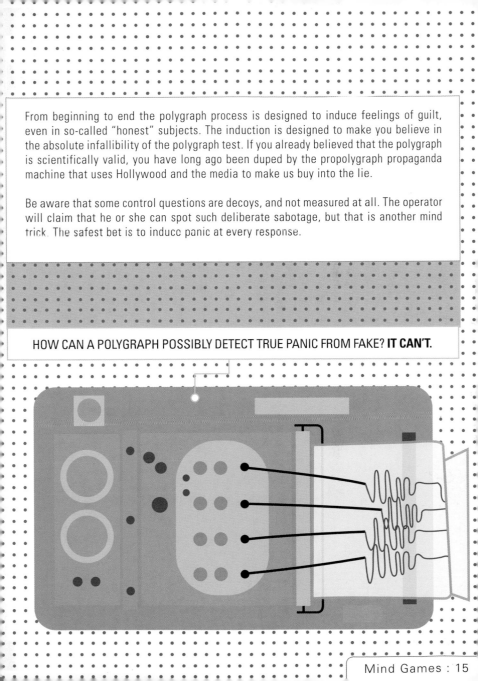

Do Impossible Sums in Your Head

You don't have to be an autistic savant or brainiac Harvard professor to learn how to do complicated sums in your head. In the West we have been taught a system of mathematics that is full of contradictions and works against our natural desire for simplicity. It prevents us from understanding the flexible and beautiful interrelations made apparent by alternative number systems.

One of these is the ancient Indian system of Vedic mathematics. Based on 16 sutras given by Swami Bharathi Krishna Tirthaji, its natural principles enable the practitioner to quickly solve all sorts of mathematical problems in pure and applied mathematics.

Multiplication

Here's how to multiply any two 2-digit numbers, e.g., $\begin{array}{r} 72 \\ \times\ 73 \end{array}$.

Step 1

Multiply the numbers in the left hand column (7 x 7 = 49).

Step 2

Multiply the diagonals and add the result (7 x 3) + (7 x 2) = 35.

Step 3

Multiply the numbers in the right hand column (2 x 3 = 6).

Step 4

Place the three results side by side (49 35 6) and if any of the results have a two-digit number to their right, working from left to right, add the left digit to the adjacent number. (49 + 3)5   6

Answer = 5256

Like any new method, it looks long-winded at first, but with a few minutes of practice on paper, you will soon be able to do these four steps in seconds, and eventually repeat the process in your head.

Quick Square

This method will enable you to square any two-digit number that ends in a five. For example, the square of 75 can be found in lightening quick time by multiplying the first digit (7) by its successor (8) and then tagging 5 squared (25) on the end = 5625.

This works with bigger numbers. The square of 725 is 72 x 73 followed by 25 = 525,625.

Time and space do not allow more than this cursory glimpse at the extraordinary power contained in the Vedic sutras. If you are interested in further study, see *Vedic Mathematics*.

Memorize a Deck of Cards

You may think that being able to memorize a random sequence of 52 playing cards is a remarkable feat, but in June 2003 the current world memory champion, Andi Bell, set a new record by memorizing not one, but 100 decks of playing cards.

He spent five hours committing them to memory and then was able to correctly answer questions about the positions of cards from anywhere within a total of 5,200. He also holds the world speed record for memorizing a single deck—a mere 34.03 seconds!

How did he do it? He recorded each card in his visual memory by imagining combinations of objects and then placing them on a detailed mind map of the city of London. He turns each card into a picture—a vivid animal or object that he associates with a particular card. The jack of clubs might become a bear, the nine of diamonds a saw, and the two of spades a pineapple. He then combines the two stages to create a surreal journey around London in which he places these objects at particular landmarks. To recall the information, he retraces his steps.

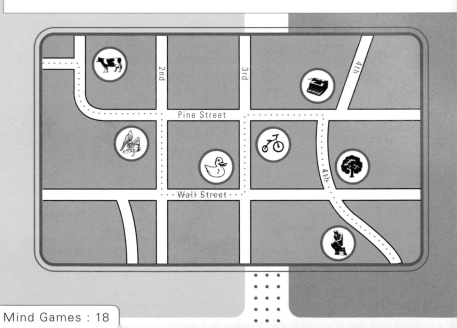

If you want to learn how to memorize a deck of cards, you must first establish your own personal set of visual associations. For example, you might see the ace of spades as a fighter pilot digging a hole. The six of diamonds may translate into a duchess dripping with diamonds being sick ("six"). Already you have a sequence that is easy to remember because it is visually rich and stimulates many more neural pathways than merely trying to remember the cards themselves. The six of clubs may become a caveman with a club being sick, and so on.

Don't copy these examples—come up with personal associations that tap into your own visual imagery. If you choose vivid and amusing images, they will be much easier to recall than boring ones.

Once you have established a personal visual system that allows you to record not only a number but also the suit, you can then start to remember sequences by placing images together. For example, to remember the sequence ace of spades/six of diamonds/six of clubs, you could imagine a fighter pilot digging a hole into which a duchess is being sick. The caveman is being sick on the duchess's back. Now you have a mental picture of this card sequence that is bizarre (and rather unpleasant), but this makes it more memorable. These extreme images form a vivid narrative—an exaggerated story that should be easy to recall.

Before you go to bed tonight, try to recall the three cards discussed above. You'll be amazed how easily the mental pictures bounce back into your head. Try it in a weeks' time and the result will be the same. Like it or not—you'll probably never forget ace of spades/six of diamonds/six of clubs ever again!

How to Tell if Someone Is Lying

You can fool some of the people all of the time, and all of the people some of the time, but a few people you can never hoodwink—those who know how to read the signs. Our bodies always give away even the best liars, so if you know what to look for, you need not let a liar take you for a ride again.

Eye Contact: A lot has been made of the eyes, but there are many misconceptions. Generally, when telling the truth, people maintain good eye contact. Liars break eye contact. However, even bad liars know that bad eye contact is to be avoided and may even overcompensate by staring you out. In some cultures it is considered disrespectful to look someone in the eye.

Eye Position: When people are accessing memories (mental pictures) they tend to look up and to the left. When people are fabricating they look down. If there is a change in habitual eye movements, it may indicate a lie. For instance, if you ask several questions and you are confident that most of the answers you have been given are truthful, watch out for a change in eye movement that breaks a pattern to reveal a lie. The eyes may even move to the door or window (subconsciously looking for a means of escape).

Blinking: Some people blink more when they are stressed, others blink less. If you notice a change in either direction, it could be indicative of lying.

Face: The stress response shows up in the face—the subject may flush or go very pale. Some people's faces become immobile when they lie, as they subconsciously try to give nothing away with their facial expressions. This is an act of concealment, which often has the opposite effect and is the biggest give-away. Another act of concealment is touching or covering the face, especially stroking the chin or nose or rubbing the eyes.

Pitch of the Voice: It often rises during moments of anxiety.

Fidgeting: Fidgeting with a part of the body or an object is known as a "displacement activity," which attempts to dissipate stress. It may also be used subconsciously to distract the interrogator from what is being said.

Body Position: If the body is in a closed position—legs or armed crossed, body turned slightly away, hands hidden behind back, in pockets, or one inside the other—then someone might be lying.

Speed of Speaking: Liars often talk quickly. They want to get the lie over and done with. They may also speak more than necessary—inventing more and more information to justify the lie and make it seem more plausible.

Defensiveness: Liars easily become defensive and/or angry. This may be expressed in hyperbole: "Never in a million years" or "I swear on my life." If someone asks "Are you calling me a liar?" you can be sure they are hiding something.

If you want to make it harder for someone to lie to you effectively, try these three tips:

1. Make sure you are physically in a higher position than they. If they are sitting, stand up.

2. Maintain an open body position that emphasizes your receptivity to being told the truth. It is a position of strength.

3. Silence can be a powerful weapon. Guilty liars often feel the need to fill a silence with more justifications and lies.

In 1972 Robert A. Monroe published a challenging and seminal book about astral projection called *Journeys Out of the Body*, in which he describes how he began to have involuntary out-of-the-body experiences (OOBEs). He found himself leaving his physical body to "travel to places far removed from the material and spiritual realities of life on earth . . . a world unbounded by time or death."

These step-by-step instructions were later devised by him as a means of controlling this phenomenon so that he could bring about OOBEs at will.

Step 1

The first step is, not surprisingly, relaxation, about which much has already been written. Whatever method you choose in order to place yourself in a state of deep relaxation, you should be free from a sense of urgency. Allow yourself plenty of time for the experience. Monroe recommends practicing to achieve a borderline state between sleeping and waking by lying down, and as you sense that you are beginning to drift off to sleep, fixing your attention on something, while keeping your eyes closed. When you can maintain this borderline state for extended periods, you are ready for Step 2.

Step 2

Focus on the blackness ahead of you. Your brain and visual cortex may still be sending mental images, making you "see" dancing patterns of light, or pictures playing out events that have happened during the day. Allow these impressions to diminish until you can see nothing but blackness.

Step 3

Now you are ready to practice achieving deeper levels of borderline sleep, characterized by the loss of various senses, such as touch, smell, taste, and, finally, any auditory signals and vision.

Step 4

Generate what Monroe calls a "vibrational state." He stresses the importance of lying with your body along a north-south axis with your head to magnetic north. Concentrate on the blackness in front of your closed eyes, then move this focus gradually until it is six feet above your body, then "turn the point 90° upward on a line parallel to the body axis . . . reach for the vibrations at that spot" and then "mentally pull them back into your head." You should experience a "surging, hissing, rhythmically pulsating wave of fiery sparks" inside your head that spreads through your body.

Step 5

Objectively observe yourself in the vibrational state, without fear, until it subsides. When you can repeat the experience without anxiety you are ready to direct the vibrations up and down your body, which will feel "severely shaken right down to the molecular or atomic level."

Step 6

This is the separation process. Think of getting lighter and floating upwards or think of rotating your astral body out of the physical space that it occupies. Don't travel too far from your physical body at this stage. Stay close. If you have come this far, maybe it's time you read Robert Monroe's book and check out www.lucidity.com. Enjoy the astral plane. At least it's one place that's still toll free.

Eye to Eye

What do you do when you don't know the answer to an exam question? Take a big fat guess? Well, that's just how your eyes operate—taking guesses—all the time. Here's the proof:

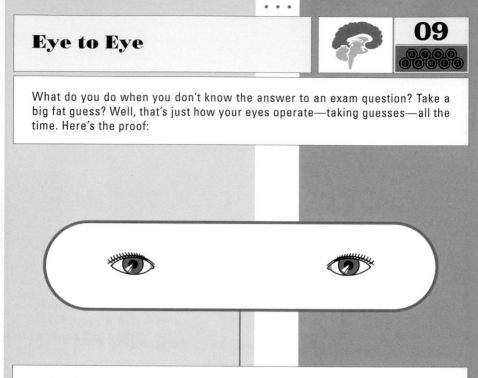

Hold the book about 12 inches from your face. Close your left eye and stare at the eye on the left. You'll be aware of the right eye in your peripheral vision. Now slowly move the book towards your face. When the book is about 8 inches away, the eye on the right will suddenly vanish. When this happens stop moving the book and take a moment to take this in. Then bring the book closer still and the eye will reappear.

What's going on? Well, this little experiment proves that your eyes are cheating when it comes to processing a certain part of the image. At the back of your eye is a thin layer of tissue lining called a retina. It is covered in light-sensitive receptor cells and it captures light that enters the eye. These light impulses then travel through the optic nerve to the visual cortex area of the brain for processing.

At the point where the optic nerve connects to the retina there are no sensory receptor cells, so this is a blind spot. This is not normally apparent because the vision of both eyes overlaps, but when you close one eye, your 2-D vision betrays the trickery.

Here's another way your eyes play tricks on you. Look at this spiral. Or is it a spiral? If you run a finger around you'll discover that the picture is made up of lots of concentric circles.

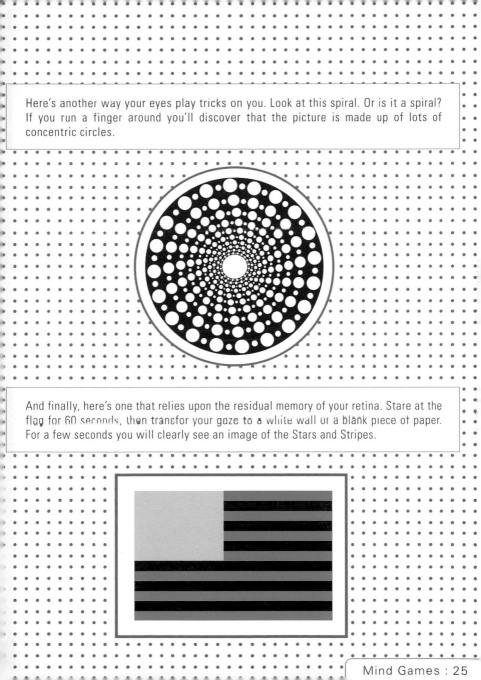

And finally, here's one that relies upon the residual memory of your retina. Stare at the flag for 60 seconds, then transfer your gaze to a white wall or a blank piece of paper. For a few seconds you will clearly see an image of the Stars and Stripes.

When you have been thinking of someone, then the phone rings and it is them, do you dismiss the event as a coincidence? When you hum a song, turn on the radio, and the same song is playing, do you shrug and mark it down to luck?

If you think you have Extrasensory Perception (ESP), there's a good chance you're right. Just about everyone has it, but it is woefully underdeveloped. Unexplained events like those just mentioned are merely a glimpse of the potential in all of us. The renowned psychic Edgar Cayce believed that ESP is a "natural ability of the soul."

According to the Association For Research and Enlightenment, ESP is "the ability to receive or send information not using the five senses of sight, sound, taste, touch, and smell." That's why ESP is often called the "sixth sense." It falls roughly into five categories: telepathy (mind to mind communication); clairvoyance (literally "clear vision"—the ability to see objects or events that cannot be perceived by the five senses); precognition (viewing events before they happen); retrocognition (viewing past events); and psychometry (the ability to learn the history of an object by touching it).

There are some simple ways that you can develop your powers of ESP, but they require a lot of practice. How long did it take you to learn to walk, read, or see your first Magic-Eye® picture? Precisely. But in order for these exercises to work, you must first accept that ESP exists. You can't develop a power whose existence you refuse to acknowledge. The more you practice and become aware of the power of ESP in your daily life, those little coincidences will happen more and more frequently as you allow your subconscious mind to inform your conscious thoughts.

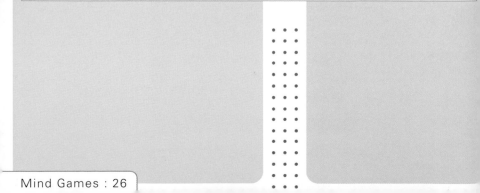

1. Zener Cards

Using a pack of Zener cards, turn over one card at a time and try to predict which one will come up next. Record your findings. For every five cards that you turn over, statistically you should get one symbol correct just through chance. Keep practicing and watch your score improve. In 25 cards, anything more than 9 correct answers is statistically significant.

2. Communicating with Animals

Try to communicate your thoughts to a cat or dog. If you are teaching it a trick, concentrate more on sending your intentions to the animal than barking orders or making hand gestures. The animal will respond well to clear, calm thoughts.

3. Pendulum

A pendulum can help to channel your psychic energy. It has been used for mystic purposes since ancient times. First calibrate it by holding it and thinking one of four responses: "yes," "no," "I don't know," and "I don't wish to answer." See how the pendulum reacts to each thought (it will swing one of four ways: right to left, back to front, counterclockwise, or clockwise). The pendulum will access your subconscious through the Ideo-Motor-Response (IMR)—minute muscle movements in your hand that are imperceptible except for their influence on the pendulum. It can then be used to tap into your subconscious thoughts as you ask yourself pertinent questions.

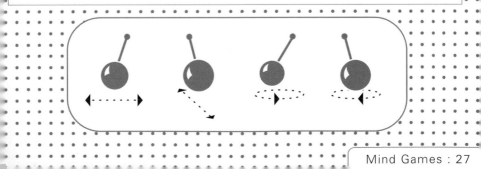

4. Construct a "Random Field" Device

A random field device allows you to see images or hear sounds from your subconscious by tuning out the conscious images that your brain usually spends its time processing. The simplest visual random field device is a sheet of white paper with a solid black circle about 5 inches in diameter. Sitting or lying in a relaxed position and staring at the circle will allow you to access "retinal feedback"—images traveling the "wrong" way from your optic nerve back to the retina. This feedback is always present, but just as the stars are only visible by night, the brightness of the images that your retina is normally processing blocks them out. An aural device could be a radio tuned between stations to white noise, which will blank out the conscious thoughts in your head and environmental noises, so that you will be able to hear messages from your subconscious mind.

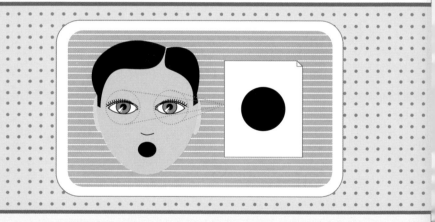

Experiment with different times of day to discover when you are most receptive. A good time is in the morning when you are still in the twilight state between sleep and waking.

Persevere. To develop ESP requires the dedication of an athlete. You don't learn to run a sub–ten-second 100 meters in a single afternoon. You are rediscovering a power you haven't used since you were a preschooler.

Think Yourself Healthy

Changing your thinking is the single most important thing you can do to improve your health. How you think determines what you eat; how often you exercise; how you react to stress; your mood; your goals, ambitions, and disappointments; the risks you take; and how much sleep you get. In short, healthy thinking is what keeps you well.

Doctors don't fully understand the link between thinking and health, but most agree that with your mind, you can boost your immune system, recover from surgery quicker, reduce pain, and live longer. In 1969, Dr. Carl Simonton and his wife, a psychologist, led research in the use of visualization in cancer treatment. Patients who were encouraged to imagine white blood cells destroying the bad cancer cells lived comparatively longer than those who did not practice imaging.

Remember those Type A personalities whom we all thought should be keeling over with heart attacks about now? Well some of them are, but you're 10 times more likely to have a heart attack if you're a Type D personality—an anxious and gloomy person who moans when he's not too busy worrying. And get this: depression actually makes your blood platelets more sticky and that means—yep, you guessed it—a higher risk of a heart attack. So you'd better think positive if you want to stay healthy.

Here's a quick checklist for your mental spring clean:

1. If something is nagging at you, find out what it is and deal with it. Take action immediately to resolve the situation, rather than worrying. Procrastination = deterioration.

2. Avoid absolutes, black and white, or "polar" thinking patterns. Life is full of gray areas, so filling your head with thoughts like "It always . . . I never . . . all men . . . women are . . . " is unhelpful. Beware of all-or-nothing terms and generalizations like these which trigger negative thoughts.

3. Do you expect the best or prepare yourself for the worst?

4. Are you beating yourself up for not being good enough? For example, have you stopped going to the gym because you'll never be the best?

5. When recalling past events, do you remember more the good things or the bad things?

6. Do you believe you or other people cause your feelings?

7. Do you give up or never start things because you're not perfect?

8. Do you motivate yourself with your wants or avoiding your fears?

9. Are you your own worst critic? Are you constantly thinking bad thoughts about others?

10. Do you believe that your mind creates your own reality, good or bad?

11. Do you trust in your ability to change?

12. Are you ruled by your past?

13. Do you value your own thoughts or view them with suspicion?

14. Can you enjoy leisure without feeling guilty or restless?

15. How do you handle criticism?

16. Are your waking thoughts usually positive or negative?

17. Do you take time to appreciate your achievements?

18. Do you listen to your body?

19. Can you look honestly at what needs to be changed in your life and begin today?

20. During a typical day, which do you look out for—miracles or obstacles?

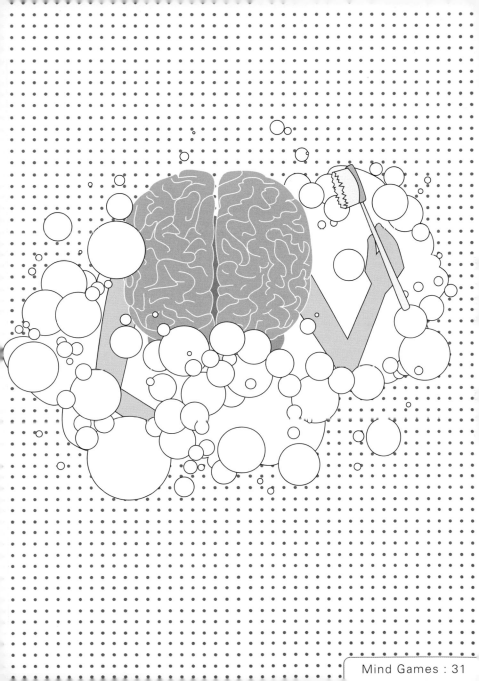

Permission to Succeed

This is not a new concept. Lots of books have been written about the way we hold ourselves back and sabotage our success. But do you really believe that? You've set goals, followed them with ambition and drive; you're persistent, and you work hard. The last thing you feel you need is permission to do anything, just some results for all your hard work.

So what is giving yourself permission really all about? Well it's different for everyone. Some people need permission to ask for help from others; some need permission to break away from their family or friends and risk doing something different; some need permission to create a new self-image that may be at odds with the one that currently "fits in" with their relationships. Here are six limiting beliefs. See which of them apply to you.

"Success is selfish."

You envy successful people so you compensate by disliking them, believing them to be selfish and goal-driven people who rarely think of others.

Many successful people are people-oriented who became successful because they helped others to achieve their goals.

"Success is a burden."

Being successful means having to work 75-hour weeks and spending lots of time away from home, which would be a disaster for your partner and/or family.

Success is a responsibility, failure is a burden. You're probably working to capacity right now, so all you'd be changing is the rewards, not the hours.

"Success is an illusion."

Successful people aren't really happy. They have failed marriages and dysfunctional children and just pretend that life is great.

Success means getting what you want (without hurting others). If you have a happy relationship and well-balanced children, that is because you have made it a priority in your life. That shouldn't stop you from gaining success in other areas of your life, too. Many "successful" famous people, such as top Hollywood celebrities, have fame and fortune and failed relationships, but only because a relationship isn't a high priority. These people know how to get what they want. They are focused, driven, smart, and ambitious. Do you think if they really wanted committed long-term relationships they wouldn't have them by now?

"I couldn't handle success."

How well do you handle failure?

The "what next?" syndrome.

You know that feeling you get after you've completed a really difficult challenge? You feel fantastic, for about five minutes, then you feel deflated. Your life doesn't feel like it's changed. You've succeeded, but all you feel is exhausted and slightly relieved. Surely there must be more to the fruit of success than this? Next time you won't try so hard, because you know that it won't make you feel any different.

Permission to succeed includes recognizing and celebrating moments when you achieve your goals. Teenagers know how to celebrate their achievements. The first thing they do after important exams is to mark their success with a party or a vacation. They turn the event into a celebration. Most of us are so busy focusing on the next goal that we forget to pat ourselves on the back. Is it any wonder you don't feel good if you don't praise yourself?

Success is modeled by parents.

If your parents weren't "successful" in your terms, that doesn't mean that you won't achieve your goals. Sure, if your father was a top investment banker, he may have taught you a few useful problem-solving and risk-taking strategies during your childhood. Or maybe not. You are not your parents. Do not be limited by their achievements. Live by your imagination, not your past.

How to Win a Game of Chess in Two Moves

Here's how to make an inexperienced opponent look like a complete doofus. It is actually possible to reach checkmate by playing two moves (that's two of your moves and two of your opponent's). It's called "Fool's Mate."

First, you have to be playing the black pawns and the player of the white pawns has to be either asleep or three months old. White starts by moving the g2 pawn to g4. Black responds by moving pawn e7 to e5. White is still struggling to regain consciousness and moves pawn from f2 to f3 or f4. Black then mates by moving his Queen to h4. Checkmate!

There's another famous quickie checkmate called "Scholar's Mate" that requires four moves.

White, as always, moves first. Pawn e2 to e4. Black moves pawn e7 to e5. White moves Bishop to c4. Black moves Bishop to c5. White moves Queen to f3, then as long as black doesn't counter with Queen to f6, white's next move is Queen to f7. Checkmate!

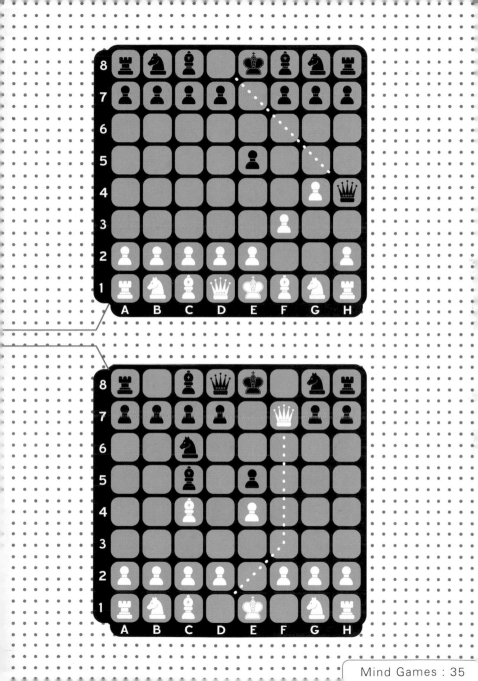

Read Body Language

If you want to know what someone else is thinking, don't try to read their mind—check out their body instead. It sends out subtle and not-so-subtle messages all the time. The only time most of us read body language is when we are trying to figure out if someone has the hots for us, but you can use it to gain the upper hand in many different situations.

The most important time to read body language is a first meeting. All relationships basically boil down to whether we like or dislike, connect or clash with another person. Whenever we meet someone for the first time we immediately begin to evaluate whether or not we trust and like them, and our body language reflects this. Most body language we pick up subconsciously anyway—ever get the feeling that someone didn't like you, but you couldn't quite understand why? Chances are their body language betrayed their true feelings.

But how often do we bother to read our own body language? We spend so much time focusing on the other person that we forget how we are presenting ourselves.

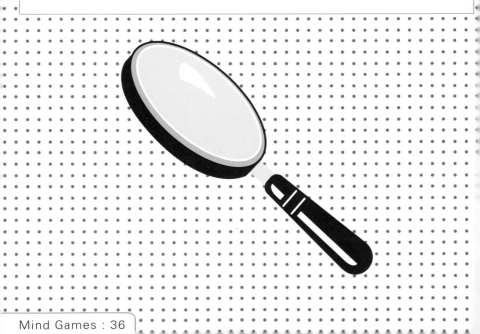

Emotion	Their Body Language	Your Body Language
Anxiety/Dislike	Looking away, fidgeting, pulling an ear, adjusting clothes, hand-wringing, rubbing back of neck, looking at an exit—door or window, clearing throat, jingling keys or change in pocket, stepping or leaning backwards, looking down, kicking imaginary objects on ground	This person feels uncomfortable with you. Make them feel more at ease by opening up your body, uncrossing your legs and unfolding your arms. Stand or sit face on and lean forward to show that you are interested in them. Maintain good eye contact and smile. Don't send negative messages by mirroring their anxiety—it may be their shyness or social awkwardness. Remain open and friendly.
Thoughtful/ Undecided	Hand-to-face, chin stroking, frowning, squinting, body partially turned away, occasional smiling	This person is still making up their mind about you. Maintain an open posture and try to mirror their more positive body language.
Interest/Trust/Like	Leaning forward, body facing yours, head tilting, smiling, grooming themselves, playing with hair or clothes, laughing, making physical contact	This person likes and feels comfortable with you. Whatever you are doing, keep doing it!

	Comfort	Discomfort
Lips	Moist, licking, slightly open	Pressed (often combined with raised chin), biting, curl down at edges during a smile
Fingertips	Relaxed, still	Fidgeting, tapping
Hands	Open, visible, palms up, relaxed	Fists clenched, fidgeting, hidden (behind back, in pockets, etc.), palms down, clinging to objects (bags, pens, keys), wringing

One of the key skills of a detective or FBI agent is the ability to extract information from witnesses of a crime. In the past, faced with willing witnesses who simply "didn't remember" specific details, investigators turned to hypnotism to help memory recall. This was successful, but ran the risk of implanting "false memories" and, therefore, became discredited as admissible evidence because it was vulnerable to flaws. So interviewers turned to a technique developed by Ronald P. Fisher and Edward Geiselman, professors at Florida International University and UCLA respectively, called the cognitive interview.

Three basic principles of this method are:

1) reinstating the context of the event

2) recalling the event in a different sequence

3) viewing the event from different perspectives

Reinstating the Context of the Event

After a brief period of making the witness feel at ease, traditional interviews would begin with "tell me what happened" or "what can you remember about . . . ?" The cognitive approach takes the witness back to a time much earlier than the event and builds up the context from there. For example, if a person witnessed a robbery while driving to work one morning, the crime needs to be put into context by taking the witness back to the events of the morning—getting out of bed, taking a shower, getting dressed, eating breakfast, their mood, opening the garage, what the weather was like, what was on the radio, starting the engine, the route to work, and so forth, so that by the time the event is reached, it can be relived in its full context, with the mood and environment vividly recreated. This approach has a dramatic effect on memory recall.

Recalling the Event in a Different Sequence

The interviewer can now take the subject forward to after the event and work backwards, encouraging them to recount any detail, no matter how insignificant. This will reduce the witness's tendency to self-censor and edit during the chronological sequencing—skipping to what the witness feels are "important" details. The interviewer may revisit specific segments within a sequence several times and deal with them independently for greater clarity and recall.

Viewing the Event from Different Perspectives

Here the interviewer asks the witness to view events from a perspective other than their own. This might involve asking them to consider another person's perspective, or to imagine being in a different place, or even in the position of a fictional surveillance camera. This changes perspective and might help the witness to be more objective as he or she plays back an imaginary film.

Other Techniques

Association with the Familiar: This involves encouraging the witness to associate the physical characteristics of—usually—a person with someone they know, or a celebrity. For example, "who else might wear a hat like his?" Memory works by association.

Partial Recall: If the witness is trying to recall a license plate number, the interviewer would concentrate on fragments—the first or last letter or number, or its shape—and build from there.

Throughout the interview, it is important to make the witness feel that all of their information is important; otherwise they will withhold "irrelevant" details or close down when the interviewer runs out of steam. An inexperienced interviewer will ask, "Can you think of anything else you've left out?" making the witness feel redundant if the answer is "no." The longer the interviewer can sustain a dialogue in which the witness feels useful, the more information will be recovered.

How to Develop Mental Toughness

How often have you heard the phrase "mental toughness" applied to athletes and thought that it doesn't apply to you? If they need it to win a race, then how much more important is your entire life? If you want to get what you want and have a healthy and active life, you've got to develop plenty of mental toughness.

People go to the gym to develop physical strength, but pay scant attention to their mental strength. Just as repetition of exercise builds muscle, fitness, flexibility, and stamina, repeated mental exercise buffs up your mental toughness. If you don't train your mind, you will never control your life, reach your full potential, and have fun along the way. The only way to develop mental toughness is with maximum reps. Here's how:

1. Don't postpone happiness or the ability to effect changes until after you have reached your goals or you will have to wait a long time ("As soon as I get that pay raise, I'll quit smoking").

2. Set clear and detailed goals and break them down into long-term, short-term, and daily goals. Motivation comes from having plenty of good reasons for doing something. If you can't come up with good reasons, you're wasting your time.

3. Pace yourself. Being consistent, regardless of the context, produces better results than a quick burst of activity followed by burn out or a bender.

4. Put in good work. Whatever your goal, practice does not make perfect—only good practice does that. Give your full attention to the matter in hand. Concentrate on the process, not the outcome. If you work or train all day thinking about how good it will feel when you've finished, you will slack off and open a can of beer too early—you know what we mean.

5. Focus on what you want to happen, not what you are afraid might happen.

6. Recognize that negative thinking has absolutely no positive benefits (that's why it's called "negative").

7. Be willing to change tactics if you aren't achieving the desired results. Insanity is repeating the same action and expecting a different outcome.

8. Ask yourself: "What would I do in this situation if I couldn't fail?"

9. Force yourself to act positively—bodily and mentally. If it makes you feel like a fake, then it's a clear sign that you really need to act positively.

10. Forget about the past and concentrate on the present. The best way to repeat mistakes is to worry about repeating them. Learn from mistakes, then forget them and move on.

11. Respond to challenges with discipline rather than punching holes in your furniture.

12. Accept that results take time; they will come, but not immediately. That said, success doesn't have to be a hard, painful slog. Put in the work and commitment, and success has a habit of creeping up on us when we are least expecting it—don't reject opportunities for success because they feel too easy.

Play the Percentages

17

All of life is based on percentages, just like a role-playing game. When you walk to the park, there's an excellent chance that you'll arrive unharmed, but a small chance that a rabid squirrel will bite you on the butt.

Do you play the percentages in your life, or do you ignore them and wonder why aspects of your life are out of balance?

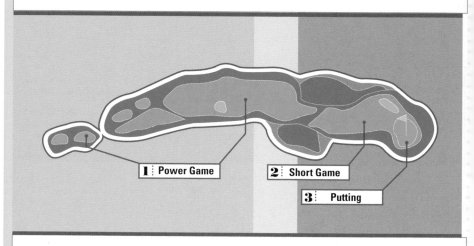

1 ⋮ Power Game   **2 ⋮ Short Game**

3 ⋮ Putting

Golf, a classic game of percentages, can be broken down into three key areas: **(1)** the Power Game (driving and iron play), **(2)** the Short Game (finesse/shots within 100 yards), and **(3)** Putting.

Tiger Woods is the undisputed master of the sport, but he isn't the best in any of these three categories. Based on the number of errors made, Darren Clark is a better driver, Phil Mickelson is better at the short game, and Ernie Els is a superior putter. So how does Tiger keep winning? He plays the percentages by being the best overall. Clearly his talent is stratospheric, but it is his all-around consistency that wins championships. What can we learn from this?

RABID SQUIRREL

1. Every task can be broken down into smaller tasks, some of which you will excel at and others which will be more shaky. Play to your strengths, but above all, focus on improving your weaknesses. It seems obvious, but it is human nature to concentrate on what we are good at and neglect our weaknesses. Percentage-wise you can make bigger improvements on a weakness than on a strength. For example, professional athletes train to shave fractions of a second off their times, whereas an amateur with less ability could improve by seconds with only a little training.

2. Happiness is a percentage game. It involves focusing on areas of your life where you are weak and paying them some attention—for example, if you feel you are a poor communicator, you could improve your ability in this area by 20 percent by, say, buying a book and teaching yourself to be better at it. If you really are such a disaster in that area, think of the improvement you could make!

3. If you drink 10 pints of beer, climb in your car, and take a ride down the freeway, the percentages are not stacked in your favor. There is a small chance that you will get home without crashing. It is more likely that you will be pulled over by the cops and lose your licence. There's an even greater chance that the cops will arrive after you have driven your car into a lamppost or an oncoming vehicle. Playing the percentages means taking responsibility for the outcomes of your actions. Most of us know what the outcomes will be, but we refuse to accept them until it is too late.

Ponzi Schemes Exposed

In the Ponzi scheme, named after Charles Ponzi, who ran such a scheme in 1920, returns are paid to earlier investors entirely out of the money paid into the scheme from newer investors. This type of scheme shows how the lure of money can fool even the most agile mind!

Join now! This amazing system really works. I was on welfare and today, three weeks later, I'm a multimillionaire!

How many times have you been invited to join in a remarkable and foolproof new scheme that promises huge returns for a mere $1 "investment" of your own money? New versions of the scheme appear every few years but the basic principle is the same. You receive a letter from someone claiming that they can make you rich beyond your wildest dreams. You send some money to the name at the top of a list and place your name at the bottom. Then you send out several copies of the letter and, as new members join below you, your name rises up the list. Within a few weeks you receive your windfall.

At first glance the mathematics seem almost plausible: Suppose you receive a list containing seven names. You are instructed to send a dollar to the person at the top of the list, then remove the top name and place your own at the bottom. You send your letter to 10 other people, and they all send their letter to 10 others and so on until at the eighth level, you should have 10 million people receiving a letter with your name at the top of the list. Even if just 10 percent of them send you a dollar, you will be a millionaire.

But here's why Ponzi schemes don't work: There aren't enough people in the world to ensure that more than the first 11 names on the list get rich. Unless you are one of the first 11 people in the world to receive the letter, you will make no money. Those eleven are the original crook and his or her 10 good friends.

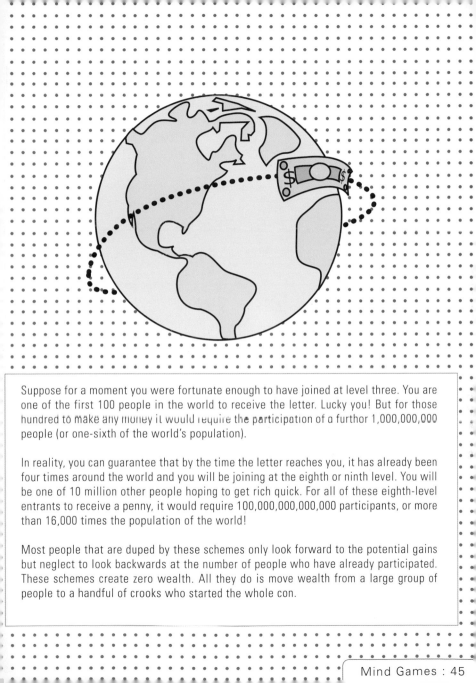

Suppose for a moment you were fortunate enough to have joined at level three. You are one of the first 100 people in the world to receive the letter. Lucky you! But for those hundred to make any money it would require the participation of a further 1,000,000,000 people (or one-sixth of the world's population).

In reality, you can guarantee that by the time the letter reaches you, it has already been four times around the world and you will be joining at the eighth or ninth level. You will be one of 10 million other people hoping to get rich quick. For all of these eighth-level entrants to receive a penny, it would require 100,000,000,000,000 participants, or more than 16,000 times the population of the world!

Most people that are duped by these schemes only look forward to the potential gains but neglect to look backwards at the number of people who have already participated. These schemes create zero wealth. All they do is move wealth from a large group of people to a handful of crooks who started the whole con.

Anger Management

Anger is a normal emotion, but a staggering one in five Americans has an anger management problem. They allow their anger to dominate and reduce the quality of their lives. If you want to keep your head about you, whatever life throws at you, then you need to follow these four rules of cool.

1. Acknowledge Your Anger

The first step to dealing with anger is to admit that you are angry. Many people suppress their anger and, as a result, become irritable, depressed, or even ill. Often suppressed anger finds an outlet indirectly through passive-aggressive behavior such as sulking, refusing to talk, sarcasm, or put-downs.

2. Ask Yourself: Why Am I Angry?

Anger often flares up when our expectations are not met. This may be because our expectations are too high or because we feel that we deserve a different outcome. Either way, frustrated expectations can make us feel that we have less control over our environment that we thought, and they are directly linked to self esteem.

Those with high self-esteem can take disappointment in stride because, generally, they believe that they exert a strong influence on their surroundings and outcomes. In other words, they believe their actions produce positive results. Those with low self-esteem believe that their actions have little or no effect on outcomes; therefore, they are more likely to become angry when a situation contradicts their expectations because it seems to confirm their negative feelings about their own powerlessness.

3. Choose to Change

Learn to see anger as a failure rather than a driving force. If you refuse to allow the destructive expression of anger as an option, it forces you to solve your problems another way. It is possible to redirect anger into constructive action.

4. Express Yourself

Poor communicators are easily angered. Violent anger is an expression of a total breakdown in communication. Violent and angry people are very poor communicators with low self-esteem. They are constantly frustrated by the apparent failings of others, and their own inability to assert themselves or communicate their feelings to those around them. Anger needs to be expressed in an assertive nonaggressive way (see page 120). Communicate your needs and problems to find a resolution. Beware of hyperbole! Being angry makes your thoughts exaggerated and only reinforces your low self esteem: "I'll never do it. . . . This always happens to me. . . . I hate them. . . . It's going to take years to sort this out. . . ."

In the words of James Thurber: "Let us not look back in anger or forward in fear, but around in awareness."

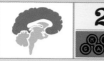
Most people know what luck is—it is good fortune or prosperity and success. Lucky people seem to have more then their share; unlucky people can't get enough; few people know how to develop it.

Remember that luck is a human construct, so it is inevitable that it errs heavily towards the material rather than the metaphysical. If you want to develop your spirituality, read a holy book. If you want to learn how to get "lucky" (filthy rich and successful), read on.

If you believe you are lucky, but the only step you take towards affirming it is the $5 a week you waste on the lottery, then the laws of chance say you are a schmuck-loser. Sure, there are people who win $200 million on the Powerball® Jackpot. That sure is lucky—no skill involved short of buying a ticket. But look around and you'll see that lucky opportunities are everywhere every day of your life, and at much better odds than 135 million to one.

Jean Cocteau said, "We must believe in luck. For how else can we explain the success of those we don't like?" Not a single person is born lucky. Some are born rich, beautiful, and into loving households, while others are poor, ugly, and unwanted. But everyone gets plenty of breaks; most of us just don't recognize them when they happen.

Thomas Jefferson was a great believer in luck. He said, "I find the harder I work the more I have of it." But you don't have to be a kiss-up like Jefferson to have good luck. Many "lucky" people do not have an explanation for how good things keep happening to them consistently. However, numerous studies have shown that these people share common thoughts and patterns of behavior. They:

- **Create opportunities**
- **Recognize opportunities**
- **Listen to their intuition**
- **Have self belief and positive expectations**
- **Have the resilience to learn from their mistakes and to persevere**

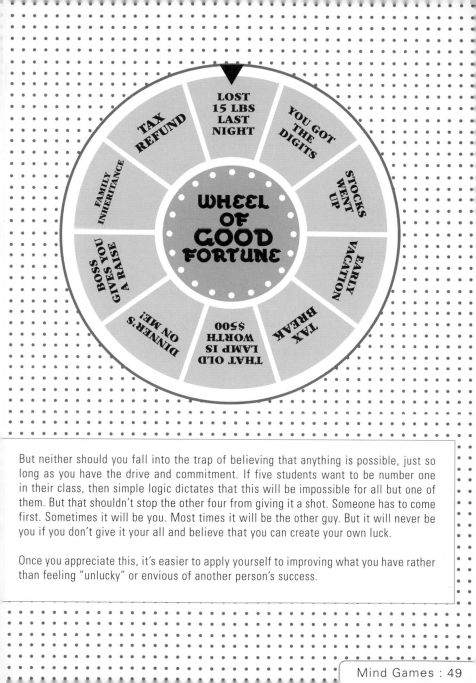

But neither should you fall into the trap of believing that anything is possible, just so long as you have the drive and commitment. If five students want to be number one in their class, then simple logic dictates that this will be impossible for all but one of them. But that shouldn't stop the other four from giving it a shot. Someone has to come first. Sometimes it will be you. Most times it will be the other guy. But it will never be you if you don't give it your all and believe that you can create your own luck.

Once you appreciate this, it's easier to apply yourself to improving what you have rather than feeling "unlucky" or envious of another person's success.

Many people think of optical illusions as a breakdown in our visual processing abilities, but in fact, as seen on page 24, our eyes are continually making adjustments and decisions in order to make sense of the world. Normally these mechanisms are invisible, but optical illusions reveal them in action.

The visual world is so complicated that the mind has developed ways of dealing with the complexity. It always seeks to find the simplest solution to a visual problem. One of the ways it does this is to group similar items together. It also tries to form a whole out of a group of objects. This is called the Gestalt effect.

This elephant illusion is a good example of Gestalt effect at work. The animal appears to be "normal" because our brains, which know what an elephant should look like, take the disjointed and contradictory visual information and interpret it as the nearest thing—an elephant with four legs. A closer look at the picture reveals something altogether more confusing.

The relationship between objects is another important factor in how we interpret them. For example, it is how we recognize the difference between something that appears small because it is far away or because it is nearby and small.

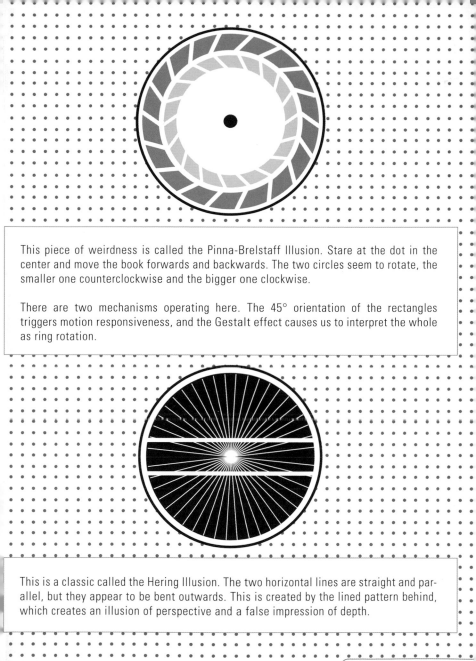

This piece of weirdness is called the Pinna-Brelstaff Illusion. Stare at the dot in the center and move the book forwards and backwards. The two circles seem to rotate, the smaller one counterclockwise and the bigger one clockwise.

There are two mechanisms operating here. The 45° orientation of the rectangles triggers motion responsiveness, and the Gestalt effect causes us to interpret the whole as ring rotation.

This is a classic called the Hering Illusion. The two horizontal lines are straight and parallel, but they appear to be bent outwards. This is created by the lined pattern behind, which creates an illusion of perspective and a false impression of depth.

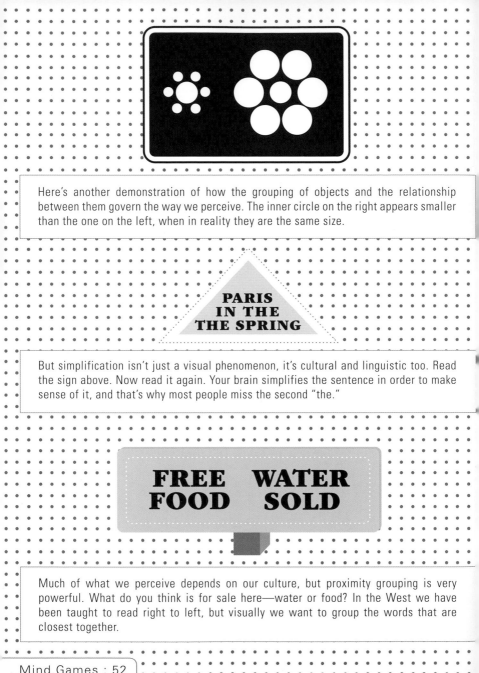

Here's another demonstration of how the grouping of objects and the relationship between them govern the way we perceive. The inner circle on the right appears smaller than the one on the left, when in reality they are the same size.

PARIS IN THE THE SPRING

But simplification isn't just a visual phenomenon, it's cultural and linguistic too. Read the sign above. Now read it again. Your brain simplifies the sentence in order to make sense of it, and that's why most people miss the second "the."

FREE WATER FOOD SOLD

Much of what we perceive depends on our culture, but proximity grouping is very powerful. What do you think is for sale here—water or food? In the West we have been taught to read right to left, but visually we want to group the words that are closest together.

The Power of Synchronicity

In the 1990s, *The Celestine Prophecy* by James Redfield became an international best seller. It claimed to contain "secrets that are currently changing our world." It was about synchronicity.

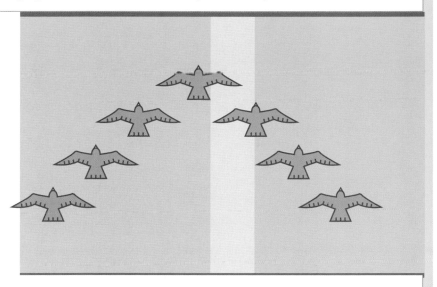

Have you ever bumped into an old friend moments after thinking about them or received money or information out of the blue in your hour of need? Have you made a difficult decision based upon a "sign" or a chance happening? Then you have experienced the power of this mysterious force. If you allow it to operate in your life, it can give you a reassuring and invigorating sense of empowerment; a feeling that events and objects in the world are connected at a deep and often imperceptible level. When we tap into the natural flow of synchronicity, our lives seem to unfold in an effortless stream of easy decisions, where events fall into place and we find ourselves heading forwards to a bright and exciting future. It has been said that "synchronicity happens when God wishes to remain anonymous."

The term was coined by Carl Jung to describe what he called the "acausal connecting principle" that links mind and matter. He said this underlying connectedness manifests itself through meaningful coincidences that cannot be explained by cause and effect.

So what's the catch? Is it for real, or new-age nonsense making authors rich by exploiting the gullible and disempowered? Synchronicity certainly worked for James Redfield—it made him a millionaire! But what about the rest of us? Can it really be the path to a more directed and expansive life?

In a word, yes. Anything that gives our lives meaning and purpose and helps us to make choices is positive, so long as it does not delude us into making dangerous and destructive decisions that harm ourselves or others.

Apart from food, water, and love, human beings need a sense of empowerment in their lives. Every day we are faced with choices. If we have few choices, we feel trapped and lacking in options; if we have too many, we may be overwhelmed or "blocked" by the difficulty of making the "right" decision. At these moments, a chance event can often push us in the right direction; it helps us to make a choice.

But here's an important proviso: you must leave yourself "open." That means not trying to overly control your environment. Using synchronicity requires you to "go with the flow." That does not mean you should surrender responsibility of your actions and your life; neither does it mean that you close your eyes and let events wash over you. Rather, it suggests that you can achieve your goals by softening your approach, by relaxing the "go-get-it" attitude that got you this far (but not far enough, right?). Tuning in to the world around you and noticing subtle patterns can help you make choices that may even take you away from your original goal to somewhere equally challenging.

It is a natural human trait to look for patterns and meaning—they give a structure and a sense of purpose to our activities. Sometimes, doing nothing is the right decision, but often it is the worst one. We turn to alcohol or TV or pleasure-seeking for instant gratification and to escape the pressure of moving forward. You don't have to be stupid or naïve to recognize that making choices is always positive because it is active. Every day many lost souls employ a personal repertoire of displacement activities to remain locked in a passive state.

Happy people are those with a sense of purpose and direction. Unhappy people feel that what they do has little influence on their life and their environment.

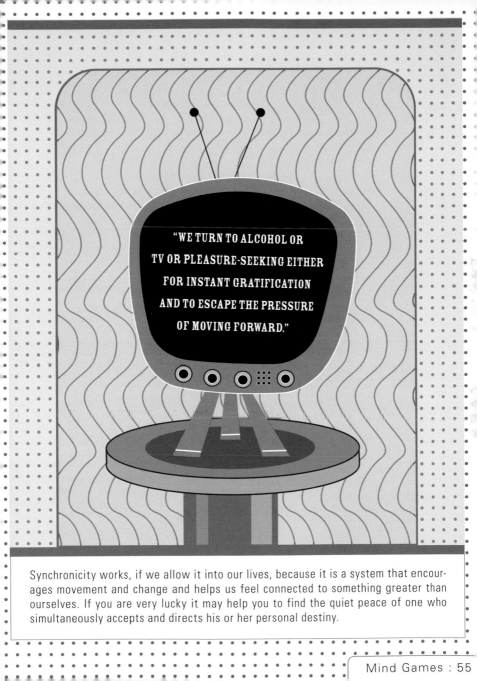

"WE TURN TO ALCOHOL OR TV OR PLEASURE-SEEKING EITHER FOR INSTANT GRATIFICATION AND TO ESCAPE THE PRESSURE OF MOVING FORWARD."

Synchronicity works, if we allow it into our lives, because it is a system that encourages movement and change and helps us feel connected to something greater than ourselves. If you are very lucky it may help you to find the quiet peace of one who simultaneously accepts and directs his or her personal destiny.

Speed reading is not magic or something that only mentalists can achieve, but it does require you to relearn the way that you currently read to correct some of the habits that may be slowing you down.

Firstly, it is important to establish that reading faster can actually improve your comprehension rather than reduce it. An average person reads about 200 words per minute with about 60 percent comprehension, whereas a speed reader can read as many as 1,000 words per minute with about 85 percent comprehension. Comprehension increases with speed because it allows the brain to see the bigger picture, to contextualize, and because a person completes a reading task quicker, it is less tiring and concentration is greater.

Here are some of the factors and habits that reduce reading rate:

1. Reading word by word. Many people read one word at a time in the mistaken belief that they must only move on to the next word when they have "understood" it. They also reread words and phrases several times before moving on. This is called "regressing." Speed reading involves increasing the "fixation zone" from single words to bigger units such as a sentence in a single eye movement without stopping. It also means reading for ideas rather than the words. Text has a flow, just like music. Breaking this flow makes comprehension more difficult in the same way that stopping and rewinding a piece of music destroys enjoyment and understanding of the tune. To reduce regression, run a finger along the line of text without stopping. This will remind you to maintain the flow and increase your speed. With practice you will do this instinctively without using a finger.

2. Feeling the need to hear the words to understand what is being read. Some readers verbalize them, hearing the text in their heads or even mouthing or speaking it. Speed readers don't do this because thinking is nonverbal and, therefore, much faster than speech. Readers who verbalize waste brain space (processing power) that should be used for comprehension and slow thinking to the speed of speech.

3. Position of the page. If you hold the text too close to your eyes, you will be unable to make a broad sweep with your eye and you will be forced to slow down. Speed readers optimize the reading distance. Experiment by holding the text closer and further away and notice how this affects your reading speed.

4. Poor concentration and moments of inattention. Speed readers recognize when they are concentrating inefficiently. Therefore, they read with maximum concentration, causing them to read faster and conserve mental energy.

5. Unclear reading function (i.e., the reader is not clear why they are reading and what information they wish to absorb). Speed readers are very clear what they want to achieve from the text before they begin reading it. For example, when reading a novel, you need to understand and memorize the plot and character development and to visualize or assimilate descriptive passages. This is very different to reading a newspaper article about popular tourist attractions to get vacation ideas, which involves understanding key issues and principles and may require little to no memory component.

If you are interested in exploring this further, there are lots of books on the subject (see *Breakthrough Rapid Reading* by Robert Krump or *Power Reading* by Rick Ostrov) and software programs for your PC, such as Rocket Reader (see www.rocketreader. com for a free trial).

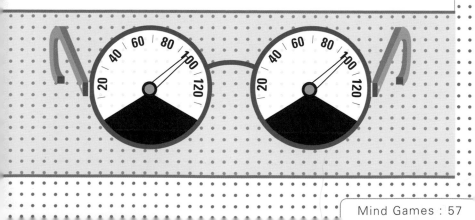

Resetting Your Body Clock

24

This is a skill that shouldn't just be reserved for jet setters who skip across time zones. We all have times of stress when our body rhythms are out of balance and need to be brought back under our control.

A "body clock" isn't just a metaphor. It's a real place called the suprachiasmatic nucleus, a small bundle of brain cells located behind the optic nerve at the bottom of the brain. It responds to the light from the eyes to regulate the body's circadian rhythms, or 24-hour cycle. Your body likes routines and so does the body clock. Mess around with it at your peril.

1. Give yourself at least one hour of relaxation time before going to bed.

2. Eat a little dairy or carbohydrate-rich food before bedtime, but don't sleep on a full or growling stomach.

3. A good night's sleep does not equal eight hours of unconsciousness. Periods of sleep (deep and REM or dream sleep) are interspersed with periods of "quiet repose"—a state of consciousness between sleep and waking. It is this area that can easily turn into a worry session, either about the day ahead or the fact that you aren't asleep. Relax—this is a natural part of the sleep cycle.

4. Alcohol or sleeping tablets may help you to get to sleep, but the quality of your sleep will be impaired.

5. Go to bed and get up at a fixed time each day.

6. Your body sleeps best when it is at its lowest temperature during the 24-hour cycle. Overheating at night is a major cause of poor sleep.

7. The internal clocks of teens are different from those of adults. As a rule, adults begin feeling tired a few hours after sunset but teens won't feel sleepy until a few hours later still, but because of school they can rarely sleep late to compensate. The result is sleep deprivation—very common in teens.

8. Avoid strenuous exercise before bedtime. It will tire your muscles, but the extra blood flow and adrenaline in your body will keep you awake.

9. Cut out afternoon naps. Save it up for the evening.

10. When you wake, expose yourself to bright light—preferably daylight. Draw the curtains. Walk outside and spend a few minutes soaking up some rays. If you aren't a morning person this will help to kick start your waking.

11. Exercise and eat at regular times each day.

12. Before traveling across a time zone, adapt to the new time at home by eating or sleeping a few hours earlier or later than usual.

13. Keep the bedroom dark, especially during the summer when dawn comes before it is time to wake up. Use black-out blinds or an eye mask.

14. Use the bedroom for sleeping, not watching TV or playing computer games.

15. Avoid tea, coffee, and sodas in the evening.

> **This section is for information only. You should only attempt to fire walk after training with F.I.R.E. (Firewalking Institute of Research and Education) certified instructors.**

Ritual fire walking has been performed by numerous cultures worldwide for millennia. The first written account appears in a 3,000-year-old Indian story, and there are reports of the Kahuna people of Hawaii walking across lava floes. Today thousands of people perform fire walks without injury every year. It is an uplifting, life-changing experience, and it can be a great way to overcome limiting beliefs about yourself and conquer fear in all areas of your life. But how does it work?

Many theories have attempted to explain the principles behind fire walking. Some refuse to believe that anything other than the power of the mind alone prevents burns. While it is true that pain is subjective, the theories below may account for the lack of physical injury.

1. The single most important factor is the ability of the coals to conduct heat. Just because a substance is hot does not mean that it will burn when touched. This is dependent upon its conductivity—its ability to transfer heat from itself to another body. The 32,000 heat tiles used on the Space Shuttle are so poor at conducting heat that they may be glowing red hot, but still be safe enough to touch. Fire walkers use dry wood coals (incense cedar or white birch produce the best results), which are poor conductors of heat. On the other hand, metal is a very good conductor (thousands of times better than charcoal). If a metal sheet were heated to the same temperature as the wood coals, anyone attempting to walk across it would suffer serious burns, as the heat from the metal would be conducted very efficiently to their feet.

2. The coals are uneven, so the area of the foot that makes contact with them is small.

3. Firewalkers do not stand still—they move forward continually with purpose, so each foot spends less than a second on the coals. Each foot has time to cool while it travels through the air before each step.

4. Blood conducts heat away from the soles of the feet.

5. When cold feet touch the hot coals, the body moisture on the soles vaporizes to provide a protective layer of steam (which is a poor conductor of heat) between sole and coal. This is known as the Leidenfrost Effect (see page 62).

6. There is no "fire" in fire walking (i.e., no flames). Anyone attempting to walk on flames will get burned.

That said, taking your first fire walk is still an amazing and empowering event. If you want to learn to fire walk, contact F.I.R.E., which is a nonprofit institute behind the global fire walking movement founded in 1977 by Tolly Burkhan (www.firewalking.com), or read *Dancing with Fire* by Michael Sky or *Extreme Spirituality: Radical Journeys for the Inward Bound* by Tolly Burkhan.

Plunging Fingers in Molten Lead

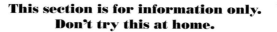

**This section is for information only.
Don't try this at home.**

If you browse through a physics textbook (on a very wet and boring Sunday afternoon), you may stumble across something called the Leidenfrost Effect. The phenomenon, named after the German physicist who discovered it, is one of the factors that enable people to firewalk (see page 60) and is the reason why physics legend Jearl Walker is able to immerse his wet hand into a bucket of molten lead without injury. (It also explains why Walker is able to command huge sums of money giving motivational corporate demonstrations—"come on guys, if I can immerse my hand in a vat of molten lead, you can increase productivity by 15 percent, blah blah, blah." Definitely don't try that at home—the molten lead part, that is.)

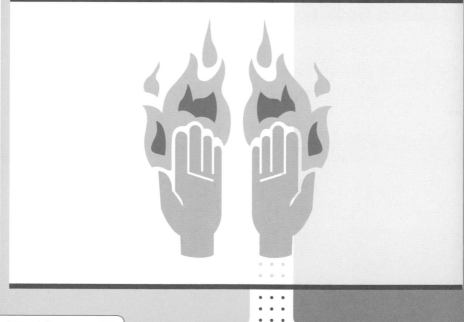

So how does it work? Well, Leidenfrost heated a spoon until it was red-hot. Then he placed a drop of water in it and watched it evaporate. It took about 30 seconds. Then he added some more. The spoon was cooler now, but the second drop of water evaporated more quickly—about 10 seconds. The third drop lasted just a few seconds. But hang on, the water should have evaporated more quickly at the higher temperature. Or should it?

It was this observation that led him to discover that many liquids have a temperature, well above its boiling point, beyond which the evaporation is slower. He called it the Leidenfrost point. Water has a Leidenfrost point of over 200 degrees Celsius. If a drop of water is placed on a surface that has been heated below the Leidenfrost point, the droplet will spread out and vaporize quickly. If the temperature of the surface is above the Leidenfrost point, something different happens: the bottom layer vaporizes immediately and stays trapped beneath the droplet, forming a protective insulating layer that slows conduction of heat to the rest of the droplet (water vapor is a poor conductor of heat). And that is why it is possible to plunge wet fingers into molten lead.

If you could bend a piece of cutlery using just the power of your mind, that would change your belief system, right? You'd feel like you could do pretty much anything. Assuming of course that you are not one of the minority of people who has already discovered that psychokinesis (PK) is a power that most of us can develop. Are you willing to at least give it a go?

Spoon bending became a global craze in the 1970s thanks to the peculiar talents of Uri Geller. But it didn't stop there. There are lots of other self-styled "pyschometallurgists" who are as busy as ever stroking cutlery into intricate patterns. One such bender is Jack Houck, a retired astronautical engineer from California who has hosted spoon-bending parties since the early 1980s because he believes that cutlery bending works best in a group situation.

Throw a Party

Invite a bunch of open-minded, fun friends around, especially children. Make it fun and exciting and informal. It's that group energy thing that really gets those spoons supple—it seems the more excitement you can generate, the more tractable the tableware becomes.

Which Cutlery Is Best?

Silver-plated brass seems to be the best material. Stainless steel is acceptable, but, according to some sources, steel cutlery is liable to snap rather than bend. You can easily find a range of old cutlery from a thrift store—purchase a variety and see which work best for you. Each one has different metallurgic properties, and some channel the energy better than others. Pick up several pieces of cutlery and you'll get a gut feeling about which one is right one for you.

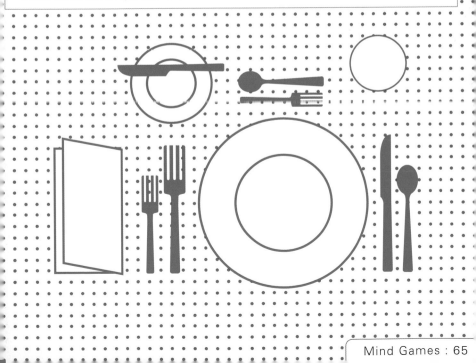

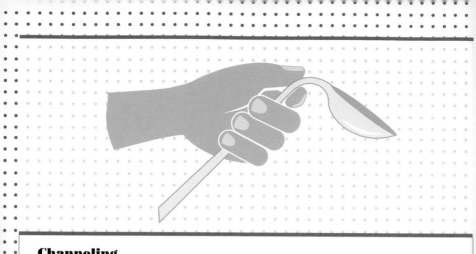

Channeling

Some benders include a channeling session before the bending. This involves relaxing your body and your mind. Imagine a bright ball of energy spinning and fizzling a few feet above your head. It should be emitting warmth and energy. It is limitless energy. Draw it into your body through your forehead and down into your body so that you feel strong, relaxed, and invigorated. Feel the warmth spreading through your body. Focus this energy into a tight ball and allow it to peak as it explodes through your fingers into the cutlery, At the same time open your eyes and shout "Bend, bend, bend" at the cutlery and release the energy into it. Feels kind of silly, doesn't it? Have fun—if you're too serious it just won't work!

Bending

Hold the fork by the neck area between index finger and thumb and stroke the spoon and feel it for a while. Michael Crichton (creator of *ER* and *Jurassic Park*) says that bending requires "focused inattention." That's a perfect description. If you want it too bad, you won't generate the right energy. Keep relaxed and don't sit quietly—chat to your friends, laugh, and have fun. The bending will happen when you are least expecting it. Use gentle pressure to bend the metal when you can sense that it has suddenly become malleable. There will be moments when the metal feels like butter—it is then that you should apply gentle pressure. You will know if you have bent it with your hands—when you are bending correctly you will use very little effort. If you are using a fork you will be able to twist the prongs into intricate spirals and bend them in ways that ordinarily would require tools—certainly not possible with your bare hands.

Most people don't know how to negotiate or don't think that it is an option. That's great news for you because, if you follow these tips, you will already be better placed than the majority of the population who think that splitting the difference is the way to conduct business. Assume that everything is negotiable, and most of the time you'll be right.

1. The first principle of the effective negotiator is to achieve a win/win situation in an atmosphere of mutual trust. Both parties must feel happy with the outcome. If you drive such a hard bargain that the other person feels exploited, you have failed.

2. Know what you want and what you are willing to accept. Also try to work out the other person's needs. Aim higher than you expect to get, and never accept less than you realistically deserve.

3. Look to solve the other person's needs. Negotiating is about building a relationship based on trust. You won't sell something to a person who doesn't trust you, and you won't get a good price if you are buying.

4. An inexperienced negotiator is easy to spot because they will either offer to meet you in the middle and split the difference, or else they won't budge at all. A good negotiator will enter into a process of give and take: giving concessions in exchange for requests.

5. Begin your negotiation armed with a list of concessions—things that you are prepared to concede in return what you want. Don't negotiate against yourself by placing all your cards on the table at the same time, or by offering concessions in return for nothing.

6. Take your time. Negotiate in a hurry and you'll be pressured into a decision you will regret. Don't let others rush you with "there's only one left" or "the sale ends tomorrow" or "I've got lots of other offers." They are dealing with you right at this moment. Focus on the terms and not on the emotional blackmail.

7. When you make a concession, always ask for something in return. For example, "I will drop my price to X if you will deliver a week early" or "I agree to pay Y if you can offer me a parts and labor guarantee."

8. Whether you are buying or selling, always get the other person to name their price. If you name the price, you risk pitching in too high or too low. Imagine you're selling a car and the buyer asks "How much do you want?" You reply, "$5,000," and he immediately says "It's a deal." What's the first thing you think—that you could have gotten more? If you had asked him to name a price, it may have been lower, in which case you could have told him that you know that your price is realistic, or higher, in which case you could have squeezed him up some more.

9. When someone names their price, repeat the price and then stay silent or say "Hmmmm"; this shows that you think it must change.

10. Shop around and play the competition off against each other. "I've had an offer of X—can you improve on that?" If you are negotiating a salary increase, know what you are worth in the marketplace. Make realistic demands. If you ask for too much you won't be taken seriously. Know your market and do your homework. Don't bluff unless you have the luxury of walking away.

11. Don't be afraid to walk away. You can only do this with confidence if you know what you want. If you don't know what you want, you won't get it, or worse, you'll be ripped off.

12. Stay objective and maintain an emotional distance.

13. Consider the total package. Price is just one of many factors. For instance, when negotiating a salary, there are plenty of factors—share options, responsibilities, company car, profit schemes, flexible hours, vacation allowance, and so forth.

14. Don't be greedy.

15. Make sure you are negotiating with the right person: the one who can make the decisions.

16. Try to agree on some easy things first to establish a relationship, and leave the more tricky issues until later. If you have already spent time building trust, your partner will be more willing to try to find a solution when the going gets tough. If you show your hand too early, it will be all too easy for him to walk away.

Think Like a Millionaire

Notice this title doesn't say "Become a millionaire." That's because actions arise from thoughts. Millionaires do not always think big thoughts, but they do think positively most of the time.

If you want to become a millionaire, it must start in your mind.

Your Internal Dialogue

This is the constant stream of thoughts that guide your day—that little conversation that you keep up with yourself inside your head. What does yours say? "I can't do that. That won't work. I'm so tired. It's not fair. I've tried that already. I'll always be poor. . . ."

If so, is it any wonder that you're not sitting on your yacht enjoying your wealth? Rich people just don't think like that. And that's not just because they are rich. They thought that way before they got their wealth. It's what made them believe they could get it. Wealthy people think thoughts like: "I can do it. This will work. That didn't work, but let's try this instead."

Millionaires and Their Yachts

Millionaires don't spend all day sitting on their yachts. They work about four times harder than the rest of us. Are you prepared to do that?

Take Responsibility

Sometimes bad things will happen over which you have no control. But you should always be in control of your thoughts and how you react to those situations. If life isn't going your way, take responsibility for it. It's up to you to change it. If you spend all your time blaming others or circumstances or bad luck, it's the perfect excuse to keep doing the same old things and making the same old mistakes.

Learn from Your Mistakes

Everyone makes mistakes. The difference with millionaires is that they learn from them and try not to repeat them.

Delay Gratification

Millionaires often have the reputation of being miserly. While it is true that some are philanthropists and others are misers, what all millionaires have in common is that they are able to delay gratification. When they get extra money, they buy assets rather than rewards. Only when they have invested in their future do they allow themselves to enjoy the benefits.

Buying Stuff

The expression "A dollar saved is a dollar earned" is not strictly true. In fact it's more, since to earn a dollar you must actually earn about $1.30 before tax.

Every purchase is a reward.
Before rewarding yourself ask:

- **Do I need this?**
- **Will I still want it next week?**
- **What are my long-term financial goals? Do I want those more?**

Always weigh the short-term benefit with the long-term gains. Do you really want that new leather jacket, or could you save $100 towards a house extension that will give you more space and increase your assets (i.e., the value of your house)?

Weigh the disadvantages of a purchase against the advantages. For example, if you buy a slick new car, the advantages might be that you feel and look great behind the wheel—it boosts your self-esteem and makes you appear wealthy. The disadvantages may be that the servicing and insurance are more expensive. You may worry more about the children messing it up (which leads to more stress in your life). You may worry more about denting it. Maybe you can't afford to move to a better house (asset) because you took out such a big loan on the car. Maybe you can't even afford the car. Do you feel richer or poorer?

Poor people spend money trying to make themselves appear richer than they are. Rich people spend their money making themselves richer.

Unfulfilled Desires Are Painful

Fear of failure arises from the pain of admitting that you want something you can't have. However, if you turn this around—acknowledge your deepest desires and combine this with an unfaltering belief that you can achieve them—you will discover an explosive and unbeatable formula for success.

Make a Budget

Do you know where every penny you spend goes? Do you keep a budget account, either on a PC or in a book, or do you wait until your bank statement arrives and get a big shock? If you have resisted creating a budget because you think it's what poor people do, think again. Use the simple accounting package on your PC—every time you visit an ATM machine or buy something, keep the receipt, then spend five minutes each day recording it in the money program. You are not doing this because you are poor—you are doing it because you want to take control of your finances.

Help Others to Get What They Want

Nobody ever got rich and happy by helping themselves. The best way to get rich is to help others achieve their goals.

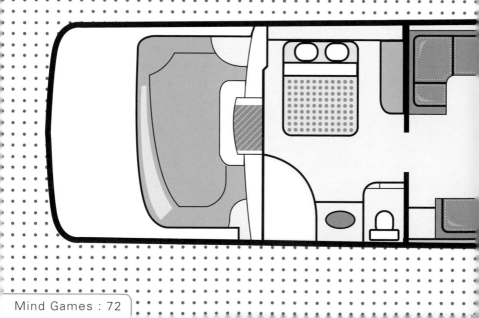

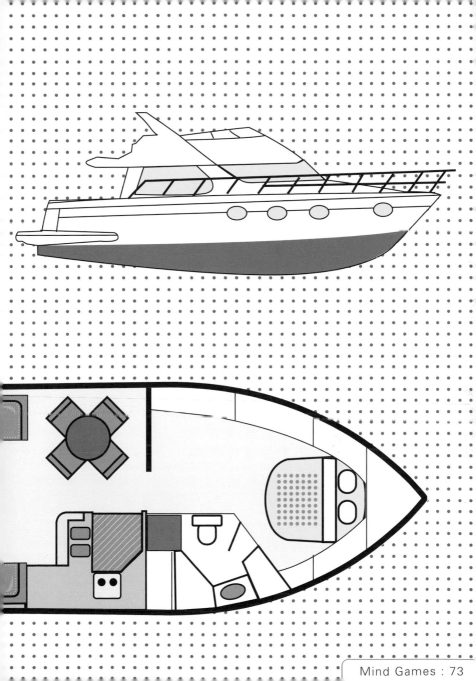

Hypnosis conjures up the image of a mysterious white-haired gentleman bending unsuspecting victims to his will by dangling a fob-watch on a chain and uttering the words, "You are feeling very sleepy."

In reality it is very different, most importantly because subjects cannot be forced to do anything against their will (with the exception of stage hypnotism in which social pressure exerts considerable influence). The Greek word for sleep is *hypos*, which is the origin of the word "hypnosis"; however, it does not involve sending someone to sleep, but rather inducing a relaxed and suggestible mental state somewhere between waking and sleeping.

Hypnotism is an everyday occurrence. For example, we hypnotize ourselves every time we watch a good movie or get "lost" in a book, becoming so drawn into the action that we can experience extreme emotions, even though we know that it isn't real. Horror movies require the ultimate self-hypnosis, or what dramaturgists call "suspension of disbelief."

So how does it work? The scientific notion of hypnotism originated with Franz Mesmer in the eighteenth century, who believed it was the manifestation of a mystical force called "animal magnetism," which passed from hypnotist to subject. Nowadays the emphasis is much more on the subject, who allows their conscious mind to step aside, in order to gain direct access to the subconscious.

The subconscious governs all your automatic responses such as breathing, heartbeat, etc. Also there are many activities, which, once mastered, you do not need to perform consciously—you do them automatically. These too are controlled by your subconscious mind. In fact, invisible and unnoticed, your subconscious does most of your thinking. Your emotions, memories, and senses are deeply connected to your subconscious, which is why a smell can trigger powerful emotions and memories.

When you are asleep you can access your subconscious through dreams, while the conscious mind is switched off. During hypnotism something similar happens—the conscious mind takes a back seat so the hypnotist can work directly with your subconscious, bypassing mechanisms such as logical reasoning and inhibition. Someone in a relaxed hypnotic state can access memories and experiences that might normally be filtered or blocked by the conscious mind.

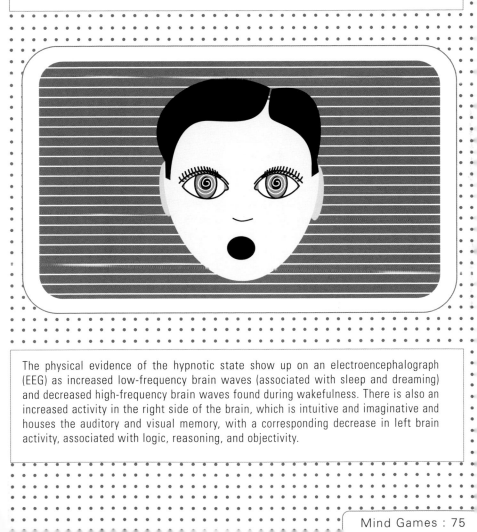

The physical evidence of the hypnotic state show up on an electroencephalograph (EEG) as increased low-frequency brain waves (associated with sleep and dreaming) and decreased high-frequency brain waves found during wakefulness. There is also an increased activity in the right side of the brain, which is intuitive and imaginative and houses the auditory and visual memory, with a corresponding decrease in left brain activity, associated with logic, reasoning, and objectivity.

There are four basic methods of hypnotism.

1. Fixed-gaze: the hypnotist focuses the subject's attention on a single point or object to the exclusion of everything else.

2. Forceful commands: this is a relatively quick method that relies on the subject surrendering their will to the authoritative commands of the hypnotist. This is very effective in stage hypnotism where subjects have the added social pressure of an audience to encourage them to obey and conform.

3. Loss of balance: this seeks to disorientate the mind and body, and can be gentle, such as the rocking of a baby, that deeply relaxes, or the sudden jolt that some charismatic preachers use to knock their subjects off balance to induce a trance-like state.

4. Relaxation: this is by far the most popular method. The subject is guided into progressively deeper states of relaxation, using visual imagery while listening to the calming voice of the hypnotist.

These methods will only work on a comfortable, relaxed, and willing subject, who believes that they can be hypnotized and trusts the hypnotist's ability, motives, and authority. Sigmund Freud's psychoanalytic couch was very effective in both relaxing and physically subordinating his patients, raising his status and thus increasing his authority and credibility—two vital qualities of the successful hypnotist.

Creative Risk Taking

31

The Chinese word for "crisis" is composed of two characters. One represents danger, the other represents opportunity.

The granddaddy of life skills advice, Dale Carnegie, said of risk taking, "The person who goes farthest is generally the one who is willing to do and dare. The sure-thing boat never gets far from shore."

A century ago those who sought out high-risk endeavors, such as mountaineering, were considered to be pathological. Sigmund Freud interpreted such risk taking as depression manifesting in a death wish. Part of this legacy survives today as we label risk takers "adrenaline junkies" and dismiss them as irresponsible and even selfish. Consider the flipside: many people try to softly tiptoe through life so that they can arrive at death safely.

Human nature thrives and survives on risk. If your postindustrial life seems colorless, monotonous, and predictable, you are living cocooned within your "comfort zone." It doesn't mean you should take up skydiving, but you do need to become a creative risk taker.

It has been said of the artistic process that the greatest artists have the ability to tolerate the uncertainty and chaos, the "unfinishedness" of what they are creating. While lesser artists seek to complete, to tidy up the loose ends, and resolve this anxiety, the great artist relishes the uncertainty long enough for something truly original to emerge.

We are all faced with important decisions and choices that involve risk, be it a change of career, having a child, ending a relationship. If you want to feel alive and deeply connected to your destiny, follow the 10 commandments of entrepreneurs, artists, and free-thinkers:

1. Be prepared to make mistakes and ignore social disapproval.

2. Tolerate being "different."

3. Face your mistakes, and the stuff that really gets you upset, head on.

4. Resist grasping for the first solution; tolerate the anxiety of uncertainty in order to find the best results.

5. Develop an accurate perception of reality rather than twisting it to suit your own laziness, narcissism, or need for comfort.

6. Stop wasting time on "inner growth"—get out there and party—meet new people every day. Keep in touch with old friends.

7. Take nothing for granted.

8. Distrust "fixing" your beliefs. Admit when you're wrong.

9. It's okay to feel confused. Enjoy the contradictions in life—tidy living is for lifestyle magazines.

10. Don't let anyone misguide you with their "personal vision." Be yourself.

32

Brain Gym®

The brain has two distinct hemispheres, each responsible for different things. The logical and linguistic left side does all the reasoning and logical thinking, processes speech, and controls the right side of your body. The creative right side controls your imagination, spatial awareness, creative ability, and the left side of your body. The two halves communicate via a thread of nerves called the corpus callosum.

Just as we are right- or left-handed, we all have a dominant side, but it is possible to reinforce the communication between the two sides of your brain. These exercises are based on the findings of neurophysiologist and educator Carla Hannaford, Ph.D., and Brain Gym® creator, Paul Dennison (see www.braingym.org). They encourage use of the whole body in the learning process for dramatic improvements in concentration, memory, reading, writing, organizing, listening, and physical coordination.

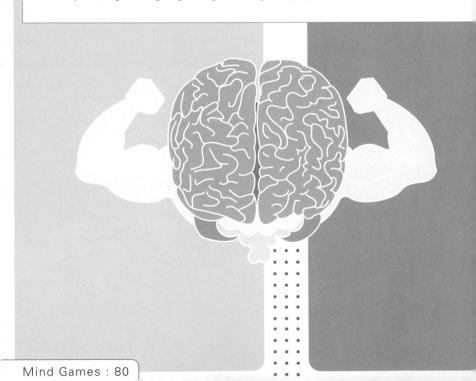

Drink Water

Dehydration is one of the major causes of poor concentration. You should drink at least eight glasses of water a day, and before beginning any physical or mental task, such as these exercises. Drinking water before a stressful situation is also very beneficial, since we sweat when we are under pressure (see page 136).

Pressure Points

This exercise increases oxygen supply to the brain by improving the blood flow to help concentration.

Using your dominant hand, spread your thumb and index finger wide apart and press them gently into the hollow just under the collar bone, pulsing gently. Place your other hand over your stomach. Press on these points for two minutes.

Cross Crawl

Stand. Very slowly lift your right leg, bend at the knee, and place your left hand on it. Lower your right leg, then raise your left leg, bend at the knee, and place your right hand on it. Repeat in a slow and gentle rhythm for four minutes.

Hook Ups

Extend your arms straight in front of you, cross your wrists, and clasp the fingers together. Keeping your fingers together, bend your elbows and bring your hands to your chest. Breathe evenly for a few moments. Cross your left ankle over your right leg and balance on your right foot. Then cross your right ankle over your left leg and balance on your left foot.

First off, recognize that sex appeal is another way of saying "mate value." If you've got it, then folks want to pair up with you. The dating scene is a jungle, but men and women are no more sophisticated in their dating rituals today than when we all lived in caves.

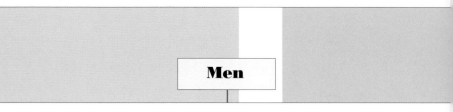

Men

Confidence
If you haven't got it, get some or fake it. Some of the ugliest guys get top action because they ooze confidence. Most of the time if you've got the confidence to approach a beautiful woman and talk to her, you're already ahead of the field. Lots of gorgeous women complain that men are intimidated by them, so they are actually more comfortable talking to the plainer women, leaving the hot ones dateless on Friday night.

Ambition
Show it. It's an attractive quality that raises your status and shows that you know what you want. Don't brag though—just let her know that you believe in taking control of your life. She might decide she wants to join you on the ride. Women are attracted to your earning potential, so even if you're not loaded—yet—let her see that you soon will be.

Grooming
Lose the jewelry and the stubble, wear the best clothes you can afford, shower every day, and use cologne sparingly. Invest in good shoes—women always check them out.

Be Interested in Her

Make her feel like she's the most special, interesting, and beautiful person you have ever met, but don't flatter her transparently—she'll see through it and think you're a creep. The best way is to get her to do all the talking. You know all this stuff, so why don't you do it, instead of "me, me, me"?

Women

Forget Pretty

Guys are visual—they're attracted by what they see, but let's face it, you aren't going to change what you were born with. That's life. Some women are prettier than others, which is a big plus for them. Chances are you've got some great features and bits you'd like to change. You know what they are and no amount of new beauty products is going to make a difference. Up to now you've spent most of your energy trying to look better. You've almost bankrupted yourself buying the best beauty products, clothes, and the rest—you've been doing it all your adult life. You know the score. There's only one way you're going to get the kind of "man you want."

Confidence

Yeah, men are suckers for that, just like women. If you really like yourself, he will too (unless you're stunning, in which case simply be approachable—otherwise he'll hate you). Period. If you're confident, he'll find you beguiling and intriguing and sexy. If you are confident and self-assured, he will think he's got to be really switched on to get you interested in him and that makes you a challenge (and men love a challenge).

An aura is the electromagnetic radiation that surrounds the bodies of living things and objects. The part that most interests aura readers is the radiation in the ultra violet (UV) part of the spectrum, which is connected to "conscious activity," such as thinking, emotions, and intentions. Some believe that it is possible to heal yourself by harnessing your aura.

A skilled aura reader can learn much about a person's character and mood by observing the ever-changing aura that surrounds them. (The auras emanating from nonliving objects such as rocks and crystals are fixed.)

Dr. Tom J. Chalko, MSc, Ph.D., runs regular lecture-workshops on seeing and reading auras. He says that by "watching someone's aura you can actually see the other person's thoughts before you hear them expressed verbally." The aura reveals our true nature and cannot be faked. It also expresses a person's spiritual development—a bright, clean aura is a sign of goodness and spiritual advancement (a spiritual leader should have a yellow-golden halo around the head). Darker auras betray more materialistic concerns and unclear intentions.

Dr. Chalko believes that we can all develop "auric sight" to see and then interpret our own and other people's aura's. It is a skill that we possess naturally up to the age of five, after which point we lose it. These instructions are a summary of techniques which he has developed to enhance this ability.

To see the aura we must do two things: increase the sensitivity of our eyes and extend the range of our vision to include UV light. This can be achieved by training our peripheral vision and strengthening the communication between the left and right sides of the brain. (The left side is linear, sequential, symbolic, and verbal; the right side is intuitive, creative, nonverbal, and color-sensitive; see page 9.)

In some respects, our peripheral vision is virgin territory—it is underused and less damaged than the central part of the retina, which is used for pinpoint focusing.

Peripheral Vision Exercise

Place this picture 4.5 feet away and focus on the dot. Allow your peripheral vision to take in the two colored circles, while focusing only on the dot. After a while you will begin to see a red aura around the turquoise circle and a turquoise aura around the red circle, but as soon as you attempt to see it with your central vision, they will disappear.

Right/Left Brain Exercise

Place the picture 3 feet away and cross your eyes until you can see four circles in a row. Now bring your focus back so that the two middle circles merge. Keep focusing on this single middle circle. When your right and left brain are working together you will see a white cross. Most of the time you will see either a vertical or a horizontal line as one hemisphere becomes dominant over the other. (Magic Eye® pictures also develop right/left brain communication.) With practice you should see the cross for extended periods in preference to the single lines.

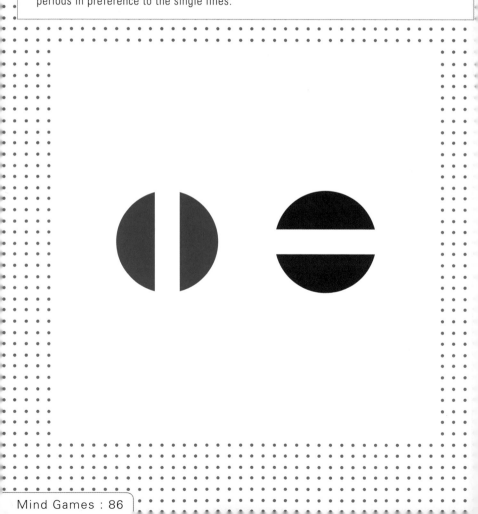

Seeing a Person's Head Aura

1. The subject should sit in front of a white background with soft uniform lighting (you can read your own aura by facing a mirror with a white background behind you).

2. Focus on the middle of their forehead (the Brow Chakra) for 60 seconds, then begin to use your peripheral vision to observe the aura, while focusing on the Brow Chakra. The longer you maintain this dual focus, the brighter the aura becomes.

Interpretation

In general a clean, bright, and uniformly distributed aura is indicative of spiritual advancement and good health.

People usually have one or two dominant colors and the thoughts appear like solar flares flashing away from the head.

Purple: spiritual thoughts

Blue: balance, relaxation, telepathy

Turquoise: high energy, dynamism, charisma, leadership

Green: restful, healing

Yellow: joy, freedom, spontaneity, generosity, humor

Orange: power, inspiration

Gold: powerful spiritual teaching

Red: materialism, worldliness

Pink: spiritual love, a balance between the spiritual and the material

Brown: materialism, negation of spirituality

Gray: unclear intentions, depression

Sulphur: pain, anger

White: disease, artificial stimulation (drugs), the visual equivalent of "white noise," disharmony

Further reading by Dr. Tom Chalko:
Auras: Seeing is Believing
The Freedom of Choice
The Joy of Health
Available from www.bioresonant.com/bookshop.html

Chakra means "wheel" in Sanskrit. Conceptually, each person has seven of these small round subatomic (cosmic) energy vortices located along their spinal column. They are physical manifestations of the soul, collecting and directing energy. If they are working in balance, a person is in good health and is able to draw upon a high degree of positive energy. Chakras that are out of balance or blocked are indicative of ill health, stress, low energy levels, and being disconnected from your spiritual and emotional potential.

The seven chakras are:

Crown (purple): Located at the top of the head and represents "beginning."

Brow (indigo): Located in the center of the forehead between the eyebrows, it is the gateway to your higher self and spiritual communication.

Throat (blue): Located in the throat, it is linked with communication and the coming together of the spiritual and the physical.

Heart (green): Located in the middle of the chest, it is associated with love and compassion.

Solar Plexus (yellow): Located where the ribcage meets above the stomach, it forms the creative center, the seat of emotions and autonomy.

Spleen (orange): Located beneath the navel, it is connected to sexuality and rejuvenation.

Root (red): Located at the base of the spine, it grounds us in the physical world.

The chakras face forward and spin in a clockwise direction and at different speeds (apart from the Spleen chakra, which faces sideways and spins counterclockwise). The Root chakra is the slowest and, as you move up the spine, each chakra spins faster than the one below.

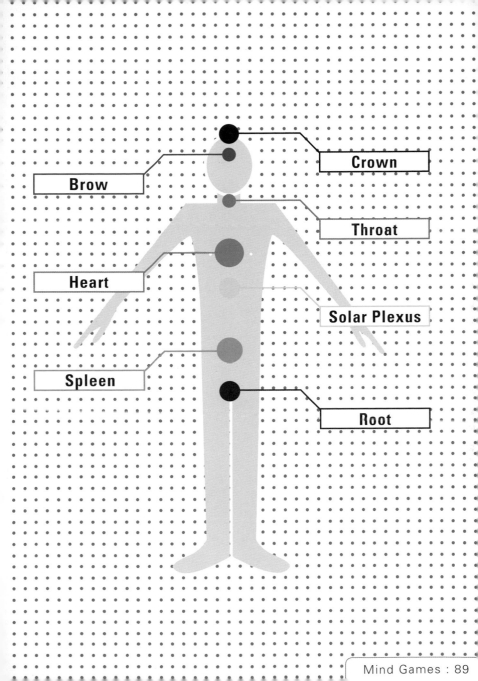

Crown

Brow

Throat

Heart

Solar Plexus

Spleen

Root

Chakra Meditation

Allow yourself 20 minutes alone when you can guarantee that you won't be interrupted. Sit in a chair with your bare feet flat on the ground and your spine straight, without being stiff. Breathe in through your nose and imagine that you are drawing your breath through your feet and into your root chakra and abdomen. Of course, the air is really entering your lungs through your nose, but if you imagine that the breath is filling you lower down, this will free up your chest and allow your lungs to open up more completely. This is not a muscular "doing" activity. It is much more about "allowing" and letting go.

The flow of energy through the chakra system is called *kundilini*. If you picture your chakras as a line of windmills, then the kundilini flows on an inhaling breath up through your root chakra and up the right side of your spine to your crown, causing the windmills to spin and glow richly with the color that corresponds to each chakra. As you breathe out through your mouth, it flows down the left side of your spine, stimulating the clockwise spin even further.

Because chakras are nonphysical areas, you must direct your mind into each one in turn to energize and open them. Continue your expansive and regular breathing while focusing on each colored chakra in turn, starting from the root and ending with the crown. As the exercise continues you may experience the sky energy entering your crown chakra and blending with the earth energy. Keep telling yourself that you will allow good things into your life. Enjoy this energized feeling of strength and protection, balance and inner peace, and hold it with you for the rest of the day.

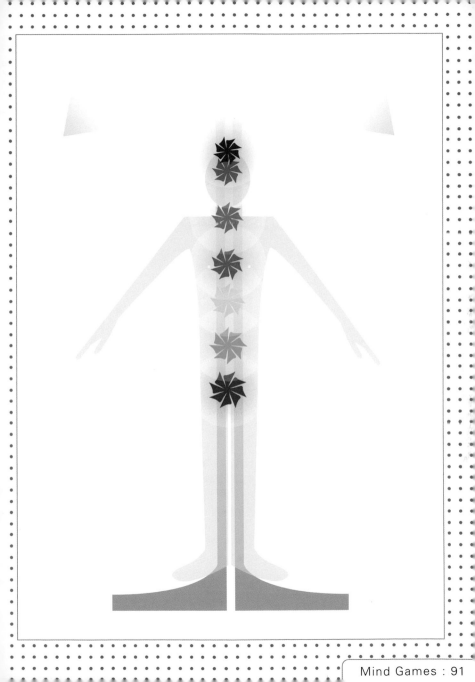

36

Remembering Names

"Look, there's what's her name—you know, her—oh, it's on the tip of my tongue."

Does that sound like you? Do you avoid introductions because you can't remember people's names? Have you forgotten someone's name almost before you've said the words "Pleased to meet you"? You need to learn these five memory tricks.

Pay Attention

It sounds obvious, but most of us are so caught up with how we are coming across—smiling, shaking hands, keeping eye contact, kissing cheeks—that we don't listen to the name.

Use It or Lose It

When you are introduced to someone, use their name many times while you are talking to them. You will fix their name in your memory with constant repetition, plus it will sound like you're really interested in them. People love it when you use their names. It makes them feel special. Little do they know that you're playing a memory game.

Association Game

Memory works best by association, and sometimes you have to be cruel to be kind. Take a good look at their face. Don't stare, but check out their most prominent feature (e.g., bald head, big nose, huge ears, gappy teeth). Now associate the feature with the name. For instance, if you are introduced to Tim and he has a lisp, he becomes Tim the Tongue, or if you meet someone called Edward who has a big nose, you might think Pinocchio = wooden boy = Ed-wood. If Gillian has a long neck she becomes Gill the Giraffe.

GILL

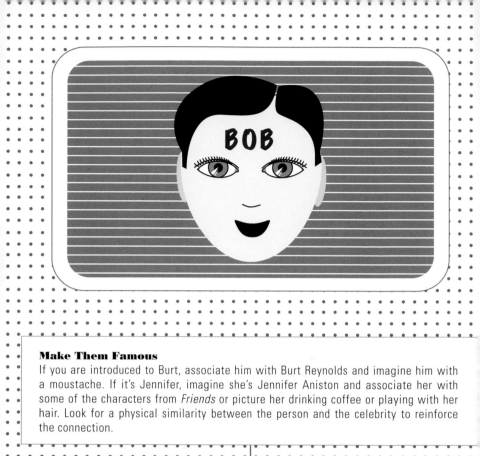

Make Them Famous

If you are introduced to Burt, associate him with Burt Reynolds and imagine him with a moustache. If it's Jennifer, imagine she's Jennifer Aniston and associate her with some of the characters from *Friends* or picture her drinking coffee or playing with her hair. Look for a physical similarity between the person and the celebrity to reinforce the connection.

Write on Their Forehead

OK, not literally. Imagine. Using the kinaesthetic sense of touch is a good way to retain information. Imagine writing the name with your magic marker finger while repeating it to yourself. Even if you have trouble recalling the name, there's a good chance you will remember whether it was long (Kimberley) or short (Ann). Or you may recall the initial letter. That can be enough information to kick-start your memory.

Ask Again

If you really can't remember someone's name on second meeting, ask them. A flattering solution is to say "I remember you well, but your name has slipped my mind."

Memorize the Telephone Directory

37

You can either do this for real (see page 18) or perform this neat mind trick.

You ask one friend to name any three digit number, then get another friend to make a few calculations with that number to reach a result. Next you hand him a telephone directory and ask him to turn to the page and name that corresponds to the result and, after concentrating deeply, you are able to tell him the name, address, and telephone number that he has chosen. Are you telepathic, or do you have the best memory in the world?

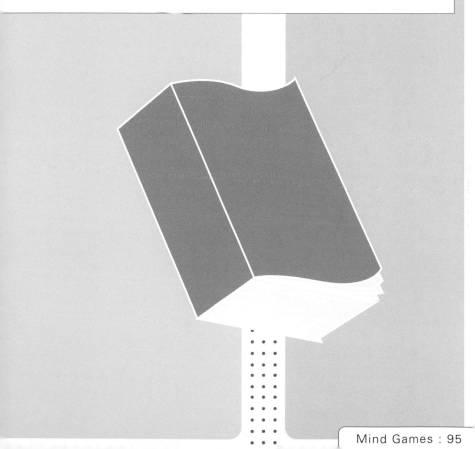

In fact, the only detail you have to memorize before the trick starts is the ninth entry on page 108 (it will work for any book—page 108, line 9). Make sure you don't screw this bit up or you'll end up looking really lame.

The secret is in the calculations. It doesn't matter which number your friend chooses, the result of the calculations will always be 1,089. Here's how:

Suppose the three-digit number was 946.

What you must do is ask your second friend to reverse the number (649) and then subtract the lower number from the higher (946 − 649 = 297).

Now ask him to take that result (297) and reverse it (792) and add the two together (297 + 792 = 1089). (Explain that if he gets a two-digit number from the subtraction he should add a zero at the right after reversing, e.g. 99 + 990 = 1,089).

You've arrived at the all important figure of 1,089, regardless of which numbers were used. (Still don't believe it? Try it now with any three digit number and you'll get 1,089; take 741 for example. 741 - 147 = 594 + 495 = 1089). Now all you have to do is convince your gullible buddies by faking the gargantuan mental effort required to recall the data.

Mind Control Techniques

38

We are all vulnerable to manipulation, and there are a myriad of ways of controlling the mind. This list will help you to recognize where in your life you might be most susceptible to having your thoughts controlled by another person or organization, your community, or culture.

Hypnosis
An artificially induced altered state of consciousness in which a person has heightened suggestibility and receptivity to direction, often disguised as relaxation or meditation (see page 74).

Peer Group Pressure
Exploiting a person's need to belong to a group can be a powerful way to suppress doubt and resistance to otherwise harmful ideas and activities.

Love Bombing
Subjects are surrounded by an overwhelming expression of love, flattery, and caring that is contingent upon the subject remaining in the group. Love is withheld if the group is questioned or abandoned.

Rejection of Old Values
Former values and beliefs are rejected wholesale, accelerating acceptance of a new doctrine or lifestyle.

Confusing Doctrine
The doctrine is so complicated and convoluted that the subject is urged to suspend logical understanding in favor of blind acceptance of its dogma.

Subliminal Messaging
Key words and phrases are hidden in a long, confusing narrative or instruction. The subconscious responds to them in favor of the impenetrable exposition.

Removal of Privacy

This breaks down social boundaries and an individual's sense of personal space and prevents private contemplation and evaluation.

Time Sensory Deprivation

Destroying objective and subjective evaluation and body functions (eating, sleeping, digestion) in relation to the passage of time by removing all clocks and watches.

Disinhibition

Breaking down attachment to cultural norms and increasing obedience by orchestrating child-like behavior.

Strict Rules

Often simple and benign, they are uncompromising and sometimes illogical, the repeated acceptance of which reinforces obedience and discourages individual reasoning.

Emotional Abuse

Desensitizing and destruction of self-esteem through offensive and abusive language.

Sleep Deprivation

Creating disorientation and vulnerability by overemphasis on mental and physical activity while withholding adequate rest and sleep.

Dress Codes

Removing individuality by demanding conformity to the group dress code.

Chanting and Singing

Reinforcing doctrine through repetition of mind-narrowing mantras or songs. Reduction of complex issues to simplistic clichés and slogans.

Confession

Exploits feelings of shame and guilt through confession of personal weaknesses; reinforces reliance on the group through the sharing of "dirty" secrets.

Financial Commitment

Donation of assets and destruction of material possessions to reinforce separation from previous modes of being.

Us and Them

Reinforcing the identity and moral superiority of the group by criticizing the failings of other groups and the outside world in general.

Isolation

Cutting links with objective pointers by physical separation from family, friends, and society.

Controlled Approval

Controlling the moral imperative of behavior by alternately rewarding and punishing similar actions.

Change of Diet

Special diets and/or fasting that impair mental clarity and emotional balance.

Guilt

Reinforcing the need for "salvation" and demanding purity by polarizing good and bad within oneself and the environment, leading to feelings of shame and self-reproach.

Fear

Stressing of frightening consequences, including punishment and loss of salvation for the slightest transgression. Also fear of banishment from the group.

39

Listening Skills

Listening is the most important of all the communication skills, but it is rarely taught. Many parents fail to model good listening skills to their children, instead offering half-attention and their own opinions, or pretending to listen so that the children will finish what they have to say and leave them in peace.

Listening requires considerable discipline, empathy, and concentration. Fortunately you can improve all of these to become a better listener by following some of these techniques and guidelines.

1. Listen with your face. Let the speaker know that you are interested by using an active expression. Poor or distracted listeners are actually so good at doing this that they signal their disinterest with those exaggerated raised eyebrows that say "I'm listening" with an otherwise immobile face and wandering eyes.

2. Maintain good eye contact and face the speaker with your whole body.

3. Stop all other activity—that includes talking.

4. Look out for nonverbal clues (e.g., body language, tone of voice).

5. Don't argue mentally or judge what the speaker is saying. Keep an open mind and empathize. Only speak to clarify what is being said (by asking questions) or to give feedback that communicates that you have understood what they are saying and feeling (by repeating back and summarizing key points and feelings).

6. Use your mouth as a receiver of information rather than a broadcaster.

7. Try to form a mental picture of what the speaker is saying.

8. Try to feel what the speaker is feeling.

9. Ask questions that encourage discussion, ones that encourage the speaker to describe, explain, or share ideas.

10. Prove that you respect the speaker's opinions, even if you don't agree with them.

Listening to children is an art in itself, since they possess less experience in verbal communication than adults, reduced vocabulary, and inevitably express thoughts and ideas that are, well . . . childish.

1. Initiate conversation that encourages them to talk.

2. Be patient. A child takes longer than an adult to find the right words. He or she may repeat a word or phrase ad nauseam while thinking of what to say next. Don't finish their sentences or guess what they are going to say, however tempting.

3. Respect their opinions rather than offering your own better ones.

4. Pay attention to nonverbal communication and reflect and validate the child's feelings. Make a habit of regularly asking for their advice and opinions (there are many household decisions that can benefit by input from the whole family).

Listen with your face. Let the speaker know that you are interested by using an active expression. Poor or distracted listeners are actually so good at doing this that they signal their disinterest with those exaggerated raised eyebrows that say "I'm listening" with an otherwise immobile face and wandering eyes.

Use your mouth as a receiver of information rather than a broadcaster.

If you're listening properly it should be quite tiring, because it requires your full attention and concentration. Listening is never passive.

You don't have to be a genius to think like one, nor do you have to be an intellectual giant or highly educated. Genius is about making connections out of your experiences that nobody has made before, or if they have, they haven't trusted their intuition enough to do something with the insight.

Art Fry, the inventor of the Post-It® note, had a moment of genius, a flash of brilliance that he followed up with action. He observed the world around him, and he combined two ideas in order to solve a problem. In the early 1970s he wanted a bookmark for his church hymnal that wouldn't fall out. One of his colleagues, Dr. Spencer Silver, had developed an adhesive that left no residue. Fry used some along the edge of a strip of paper and his bookmark worked. Later he made another mental leap when he used the same technique to stick a temporary note to a work file, and he also noticed that his bookmark was attracting the attention and interest of his coworkers. He realized that he had invented a new way to communicate and organize information.

He didn't invent the glue—his colleague did that. He didn't invent paper—the ancient Egyptians did that. What he did was solve a problem in an original way by combining two ideas for the first time.

Bette Nesmith Graham was a bad typist who developed a method for hiding her mistakes. She used white tempura paint, which she later began to sell to other secretaries and office workers. Her Liquid Paper® was bought two decades later by Gillette Corporation for $47.5 million plus royalties.

Below are some observations about the way a genius experiences the world and some simple ways to transform your own thought processes.

1. Try to view your problems as gateways to success.

2. When you perceive a new connection between two ideas, notice it and explore its significance. A connection can be a similarity or a comparison.

3. Our brains make connections all the time. It is how we make sense of the world. A genius is someone who has developed a complex and densely layered system of connections.

4. A genius can look at specifics and make generalizations to analyze the structures that lie behind them.

5. A genius relishes the play of the mind—what others might call daydreaming. Exploring new areas of thought can seem unproductive in a goal-oriented world that places so much importance on results, getting things done, and earning money. A genius is happy to spend a lot of time exploring the process rather than trying to find a result. Lose yourself in an idea. Become so engrossed that you lose track of time. That's the only way to truly create and be instinctive.

6. Develop your curiosity and sense of wonder at the deep mystery of life. No one ever explored without curiosity.

7. Keep your ideas simple and beautiful.

8. Broaden your interests. A genius is passionately devoted to his or her field of expertise, but has a myriad of other interests and knowledge areas that inform and feed into it.

9. Resist the urge to dismiss information that doesn't fit with what you already "know." Try to build bridges between your existing knowledge and unfamiliar ideas.

10. Transform your thoughts into actions. Sometimes the most obvious thoughts are the most original, but we ignore them because we think that someone must have already thought them. We think up a great idea, but it is so simple, so fresh, so obvious that we think, "Nah—someone is already doing that." Well, are they? What makes you so sure?

41

The Mozart Effect®

Wolfgang Amadeus Mozart was born in Salzburg, Austria, in January 1756. When he died a short 35 years later, he left a body of chamber music, orchestral works, and operas that is unsurpassed in its transcendent beauty, emotional subtlety, and expressive complexity.

Nearly 250 years after his birth, his music has sparked a controversial debate about its ability to improve cognitive and spatial perception. This phenomenon is now known throughout the world as the Mozart Effect®.

In 1993 at the University of California (UC), physicist Gordon Shaw and Frances Rauscher, a former concert cellist, conducted an experiment. They used 84 college students to show that listening to the first 10 minutes of the Mozart Sonata for Two Pianos in D Major (K. 448) improved spatial-temporal reasoning ability. The effects were significant, though temporary (they lasted an hour). Ever since, the Mozart Effect® has exerted a powerful grip on the public imagination, largely as a result of the marketing prowess of Don Campbell, who has trademarked the name and has been promoting his best seller *The Mozart Effect: Tapping the Power of Music to Heal the Body, Strengthen the Mind and Unlock the Creative Spirit*, and a raft of other related products ever since. But can listening to Mozart really improve your mind?

From direct marketers to legislators and educators, everyone is prepared to give Wolfgang the benefit of the doubt (despite the fact that he died in poverty and was always plagued with ill health—maybe he listened to too much death metal). And it hasn't stopped there. In 1998 two Florida legislators proposed that state-funded child-care centers expose their children daily to Beethoven. It is worth bearing in mind that the UC study was very limited in its scope, although much research has been conducted to show links between improved IQ and the learning of a musical instrument.

Ah, what's the harm? If you want to improve your IQ, if only for a few hours, slap some Mozart on the hi-fi and go and prune your roses, or indulge in a spot of topiary, while your spatial awareness is at its peak. More importantly, encourage your child to take up a musical instrument, and why not start those piano lessons you always wished you'd had? Learning to play a musical instrument or to sing may bring an intellectual edge to members of your household even though it may amuse or annoy your neighbors!

42

How to Win at *Jeopardy*®

You watch it every day and are certain you could take on those big winners in front of 17 million viewers. It's your destiny. You just know you've got what it takes. You should definitely give it your best shot, but it pays to be prepared. Here are 12 tips for landing a big bunch of cash.

1. Spend at least a year watching the show and systematically improving your knowledge and recall before you even audition. If you pass the audition but haven't prepared, you won't perform to your best when you find yourself on TV within a few weeks.

2. If you know the answers, but can't recall them fast enough, then you need to work on your recall ability. This means reviewing what you already know so that it is fresh in your memory. If you don't know the answers, you must improve your knowledge.

3. Watch the show daily and keep score. Draw two six-by-five grids and write the category headings at the top of each column. Double check the square for a correct answer that beats the contestants on TV, a single check for a slow but correct answer, and mark an X for when you didn't have a clue. This will enable you to see your subject areas of weakness, and spot whether you need to work on your recall or knowledge base.

4. Only audition when you can consistently score around $28,000. However, bear in mind that it is easier to answer questions when you are relaxed at home than it is on TV under stress. If you are prone to nerves, wait until your score is $32,000 or even $36,000.

5. You must know: state and world capitals; United States presidents (order, years of office, and personal details); state nicknames; Shakespeare's plays—basic plot lines and major characters; history; geography; literature; mythology; artists; composers; religions; and languages.

6. Popular culture, show biz, and sports will appear in the first round, where there's much less money at stake, but they won't get you much further.

7. Learn to recognize the clue in the questions. A lot of these clues consist of a nationality and an occupation. For example, if you hear: Swedish playwright, it's usually Strindberg; a Norwegian playwright will be Ibsen; a Polish composer will be either Chopin or Paderewski; a Welsh poet is Dylan Thomas, and so forth.

8. After you've watched many episodes, you'll recognize that the same stuff comes up again and again in different forms. Pay special attention to Double and Final Jeopardy to spot patterns in material, style, and phrasing for these big money questions.

9. During the audition, be a good contestant and create a positive impression: speak clearly, look lively, and have fun. Above all, do what the contestant coordinators say. You won't be selected if you can't follow instructions, if you are verbally or vocally inept, or if you look like you'd double cross your grandma to grab the prize money.

10. At home, try to anticipate the studio atmosphere. One way is to shine bright lights on you to simulate studio lighting. You can simulate stress by playing the radio loud while you watch TV. This will rob you of vital brain space and make you aware of how loss of focus can destroy your concentration. Winners can control their nerves and filter distractions.

11. Read the question to yourself faster than Alex Trebek is speaking. That way you can think of the answer before he has finished, and you can concentrate on pressing the buzzer correctly.

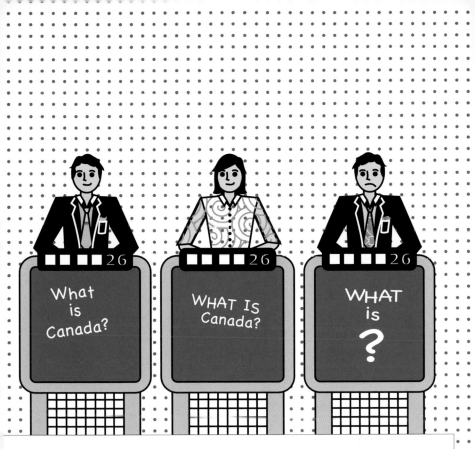

12. You are told by the program coordinators to only press the buzzer after the small pin lights in the middle of panels surrounding the playing board have lit up. Don't. Instead, time it to when Alex finishes speaking, after which an assistant off stage presses a button that unlocks the buzzers. If you press too soon you will be locked out for a split second, so it's important to time your first press of the buzzer correctly, then keep on pressing it as many times as you can. This is because you may have been locked out the first time, but can win on subsequent attempts if the other contestants were locked out too.

This is a powerful way of solving problems or generating new ideas. This method forces you to find a solution to a problem by finding a bridge between two random words, ideas, or pictures. It's also great practice for solving logic puzzles and brainteasers.

The key to brainstorming and thinking laterally is generating new contexts for established patterns. For example, the brainteaser "Romeo and Juliet are lying dead in a pool of water and broken glass—what happened?" only makes sense if you change the context of the two protagonists by acknowledging that non-human animals (i.e. goldfish) may also have names.

Random association is effective because it forces you to alter the context within which you normally view a particular situation or problem.

Here's how it works: Choose a random word from a dictionary or visit www.randomwordgenerator.com/websoftware.html to generate one. Don't cheat. You must use the word that you are given, even though it may seem absurd, and then form associations to bridge the gap between it and an idea you wish to explore.

Essential rules for brainstorming are:
• **Do not criticize or censor your ideas**
• **Explore a large quantity of ideas**
• **Use an idea to build to another**
• **Invent wild, silly, and over-the-top ideas**

Brainstorming Example #1

Imagine you wanted to explore new ideas about paper.
Your random word is "toaster."

A bridging idea could be that a toaster pops up the toast when it is ready.

The resulting final idea could be to design a dispenser that shoots out pieces of notepaper for writing messages

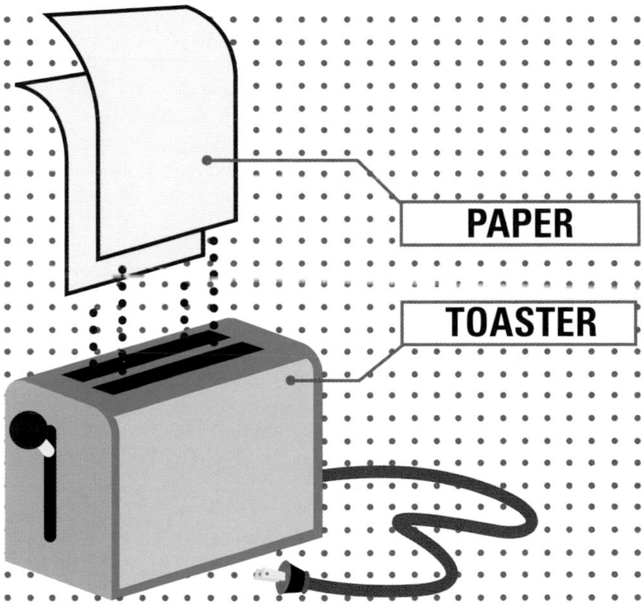

PAPER

TOASTER

Creative potential energy

Potential energy is defined as the stored energy that an object possesses by virtue of its position with respect to other objects. For example if you pick up a ball and hold it above your head, the ball gains potential energy because if you drop it, it will fall to the ground. You created this energy by altering the position of the object. You can use random association to generate "creative potential energy" because it alters the position of an object with respect to other objects in a cognitive system. It builds creative potential energy into this system, so that even if you are a predominantly left-brained person who thinks things through logically, you will achieve a creative solution because random association builds creative potential energy into the system.

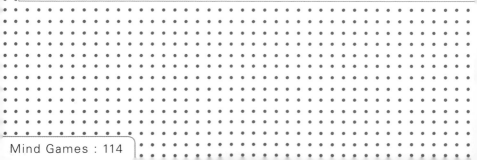

Brainstorming Example #2

Using a random word of "mustache" in the context of new ideas about dinosaurs.

A bridging idea could be a dinosaur called a "Grouchosaurus," complete with cigar, glasses, and long ribbed tail. That might set you thinking of other mustache-wearing animals.

The resulting final idea could be a children's picture book featuring a fancy dress party where all the animals come dressed up as people.

As you practice this technique you may unlock many area of your life that were closed before because you censored your thoughts or reasoned in conventional ways. Using random association means you need never be stuck for ideas again.

Super Strength

How we think can greatly influence our physical strength. There are reports of ordinary people demonstrating impossible feats of strength during moments of crisis—for example, parents lifting vehicles with their bare hands to rescue children trapped underneath. Adrenaline and the mind are a formidable combination.

Here are three tricks that are more about leverage than the power of the mind, but you needn't tell your victims that. Just let them believe that you have a will of steel.

Head Case

Sit on the floor with your legs crossed. Put your dominant hand on top of your head with the palm face down. Spread your fingers wide. Now ask a friend to grip your arm at the elbow and attempt to remove your hand from your head. They will find it almost impossible.

Secret: Your arm is a lever and the powerful parts of any lever are the ends. Your elbow is the fulcrum, so any attempt to exert force here will be easily matched by the leverage in your arm. It is the equivalent of trying to open a door by pressing on the hinges.

Chair Control

Ask your friend to sit in a straight backed chair with his knees pressed together, feet flat on the floor, and his hands holding the edge of the seat. Now stand in front of him and place your middle finger in the middle of his forehead. Begin to breathe deeply and make a big show of focusing your mental energy. When you are ready, invite him to attempt to stand up. Explain that he will find it impossible, since you are using your psychic energy to keep him pinned to the chair.

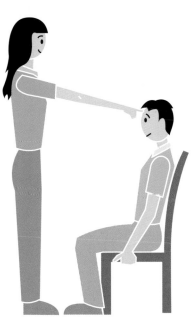

Secret: In order for him to stand up he must move his center of gravity in front of his knees, but he can't do that with his backside stuck at the back of the chair.

Sistene Chapel

Stand in a suitably Zen-like state with elbows and knees slightly bent and your two index fingertips touching in front of your chest. Ask your friend to face you at arms' length, grip you by each wrist, and attempt to pry your fingers apart. Because of your trance-like state, he will be unable.

Secret: Because his arms are straight, he won't be able to use the same leverage that you can with your bent arms. Also, you are using a stronger set of muscles.

How to Be Assertive

Many people mistake being assertive for being aggressive. They act aggressively and then wonder why other people think they're a loser with high blood pressure. Aggressive behavior involves expressing your wants in a way that kicks other people where it hurts, using threats or put-downs. Assertive behavior means expressing your needs and communicating them in a direct way while respecting the views and needs of others—unless they're complete wimps, of course.

Others avoid being assertive because they do not want to make themselves unpopular. In the long run, honesty expressed with empathy is more powerful, likeable, and worthy of respect than meek acceptance of a situation in order to keep the peace and be "liked."

So how is it done? Here are 10 steps to being more assertive.

1. Keep calm. Anger is a sign of weakness, not strength. Assertive people control their own emotions before attempting to influence others. If you feel angry and nervous, the best way to conquer these emotions is to express your needs clearly and calmly. If someone is angry with you, listening is the best way to diffuse it. If the other person does not calm down, walk away and talk to them later.

2. Mirror your words with your body language (i.e., keep eye contact, speak clearly and audibly, maintain an open posture) and do not follow your opinions with a string of excuses. A simple honest explanation should be enough. Use phrases such as "I won't" or "I've decided not to," which emphasize that you have made a choice, rather than "I can't," which implies you are powerless.

3. Apologizing for a refusal may seem like an effective sweetener, but it often weakens your position, and gives the other person a chance to exploit possible feelings of guilt. For instance, if you receive a sales call from a company asking if they can spare a moment of your time, saying "No, but thank you for calling. Goodbye," is a polite and assertive way of ending further communication, whereas saying "No, sorry, I'm very busy at the moment . . ." gives the caller the option of asking "May I call you later?" which will probably result in another excuse from you: "No, sorry." You end the conversation feeling guilty, exploited, and irritated.

4. Acknowledge that you have the right to change your mind.

5. Be clear with yourself about what you want. You can't stand up for your needs if you aren't clear what they are.

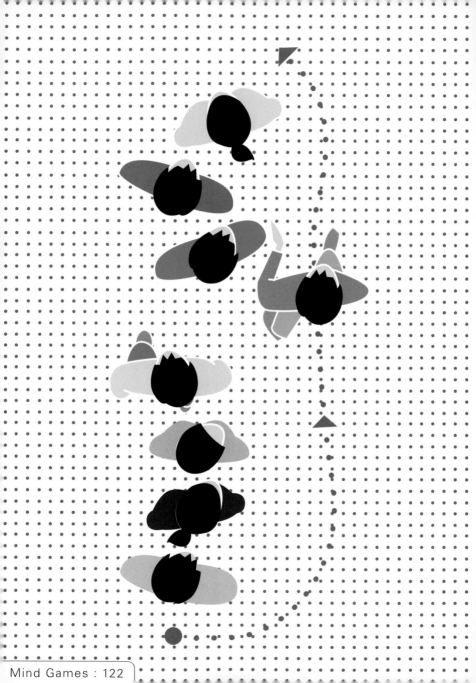

6. Don't be afraid to be different and to stand out from the crowd. The urge to conform prevents many people from expressing their needs.

7. Everyone has different opinions, and this inevitably causes conflicts. Accept that they are a natural part of life.

8. Be prepared to compromise, but not to the point of feeling exploited. Often a win-win situation, where both parties feel satisfied with the outcome, is achievable.

9. If you do not have enough information to make a decision, ask questions and clarify your position. Take your time and do not be bullied into making hasty decisions.

10. Assertive behavior seeks to restore a power imbalance within a relationship. It does not look to "win at all costs."

You've probably read most of these 20 tips somewhere or other, but how many of them do you put into practice when you're studying? Use them—they really work, you know.

1. Designate an area for study only, and always study in the same place. It should be free from clutter and distractions, well-lit, ventilated, and at a comfortable temperature. Don't study in bed because your mind and body associate it with sleeping. Also, when you recall the information, you won't be in bed! Study and recall environments should be similar for maximum recall.

2. Before you begin a study session, spend five minutes breathing deeply while clearing your head of daily clutter, otherwise your mind will wander onto unfinished business, unpaid bills, errands that need running, and people who need phoning.

3. Put on your thinking cap! Good study is about creating positive habits. If you associate a particular item of clothing with studying (e.g., a hat, a jumper, shoes), it will be another re-enforcer that tells you "now I am studying." Rituals aid concentration. Unfortunately, these same rituals can easily become time wasters—making a cup of coffee, having a cigarette.

4. Establish your optimum concentration span (the time you can study without your mind wandering) and break your study periods into multiples of this unit with 10-minute breaks in between.

5. Set aside a unit of time for a study period and dedicate it 100% to study and nothing else. If you allow any distractions they will quickly multiply (e.g., checking e-mails, making coffee, opening mail). Study in short intensive bursts. Try to study at the same time every day.

6. BEGIN. It's the best way to finish! Time spent before beginning is time spent worrying.

7. Don't over-commit yourself. One hour of maximum concentration is more effective and less tiring than three hours of mind wandering.

8. Break your workload into small tasks, otherwise you will be overwhelmed by the overall volume of material. Create a realistic schedule and focus on one day's study at a time. Break each day into small units.

9. Set goals—understand the overall goal of your study. If it is passing an examination, look beyond that goal to the super-objective—getting into college, getting a promotion. Poor goal-setting leads to "that'll do" syndrome.

10. Do important or difficult stuff first while you are fresh.

11. Test yourself. It is the only way to check that you have understood and retained information. Approach the material from many different angles and create many associations between individual items.

12. Something half-learned isn't learned at all.

13. If you are bored, switch tasks.

14. Do rote memory learning before you fall asleep for the night.

15. Little but frequent studying results in better recall than studying the night before.

16. Distinguish between what you need to learn verbatim and concepts that need to be understood. Don't be lazy and mix up the two.

17. If your mind wanders, take a five minute break, stand up, and leave the room; otherwise you will create an association between the study area and poor concentration.

18. Make completion of individual tasks your biggest reward while studying. Only allow yourself a physical reward at the end of the session, otherwise the rewards (chocolate bar, glass of wine, a jog, cup of coffee) become distractions rather than motivators.

19. Make a clear distinction between study and relaxation, otherwise they will merge into one another. You'll soon find yourself eating into relaxation time with extra studying (or vice versa) or ruining relaxation time by worrying about studying.

20. Schedule eight hours of sleep into your study timetable—write it down.

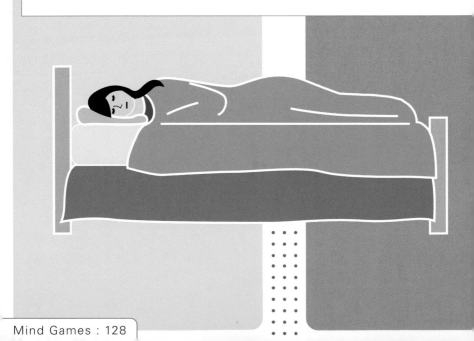

Most of us have had a lucid dream. It happens when you realize that you are dreaming and it often means that you can influence events and act out some of your wildest fantasies with utter freedom, confident that there will be no social or physical consequences because you will shortly wake up in your bed, safe and sound. As dreams go, these really rock.

Unfortunately they are quite rare, and sometimes it's possible to go on a wild wish fulfillment lucid rampage, kissing your best friend's wife, joy-riding in a Ferrari, and insulting your boss, only to find that you can't wake up at will. You begin to suspect that you aren't dreaming after all. The dream quickly becomes a nightmare.

Fortunately, lucid dreaming is easier than you think and is a skill you can develop, like learning a new language. It is also possible to use it for good (rather than antisocial mayhem!)—rehearsing success in waking life, problem solving, healing, or transcendental awareness. It's the ultimate creative visualization.

1. Keep a dream diary

As soon as you wake and the dream is still fresh in your mind, write it down in a dream diary. Remembering dreams helps you to recognize the patterns and clues that signal to you that you are dreaming. You should be consistently recording (and therefore remembering) at least one dream each night.

2. Test your waking reality

The best way to recognize when you are dreaming is to test your reality when awake. One way is to look at a piece of text or a digital watch and then turn away. In a dream it is likely that the text or numbers would change or something abnormal might happen on second viewing, whereas in waking reality they do not. While awake, consciously perform an act that in a dream you would find difficult. For example, some people find that when they try to throw a ball in a dream, it sticks to their hand. Be aware as you throw the ball in your waking state what "reality" feels like. Then next time you throw a ball in your dream and it sticks to your hand, you may become lucid.

3. Imagine you are dreaming

This is the reverse of the last exercise. In your waking state, imagine what a current situation would be like if you were dreaming. Your subconscious will throw up many unusual images and cues that you can then recognize when you really are dreaming.

4. Visualize a dream activity

While awake, decide on an activity you would like to perform next time you have a lucid dream and visualize it.

5. Be a dream detective

Strange things always happen in dreams, but often the same kinds of things happen. Personal dreamscapes include common unusual features—misplaced objects, transformations. For instance, you might find that your car always breaks down or the refrigerator is often in the wrong place—odd things that normally you would accept in a dream, unless you have trained yourself to spot them. Your dream diary will help you to identify your personal dream clues, so like a detective you can have an "a-ha" moment that triggers lucid dreaming.

6. Intention

This is the most important skill of all. You must single-mindedly reinforce your intention to have a lucid dream. Before sleeping repeat in your mind "this time I will remember I am dreaming" 50 times.

With motivation and dedication you will increase your ability to lucid dream, something some of us haven't done since we were adolescents. If you want to explore this further, the Lucidity Institute (www.lucidity.com) offers workshops, lectures, conferences, and electronic devices to help people achieve a lucid dream state. Sweet dreams!

Acupressure

This ancient healing art was developed in Asia more than 5,000 years ago. It is an effective way of releasing energy blockages in the body and a powerful cornerstone of preventative medicine and maximizing your brain power.

It uses the same principles as Acupuncture—targeting acupoints called Meridians that lie on energy pathways in the body—but it uses pressure (from the hands, fingers, thumb, or knuckles) rather than needles to stimulate the body's energy.

When acupoints, or Meridians, become blocked, you experience pain or physical discomfort, and there is a strong impact on emotional well-being and energy levels. Much tension and blockage occurs in the neck and shoulders. A few minutes of acupressure can have immediate benefits, and the cumulative effect of doing these exercises will leave you feeling more energized, mentally alert, and positive.

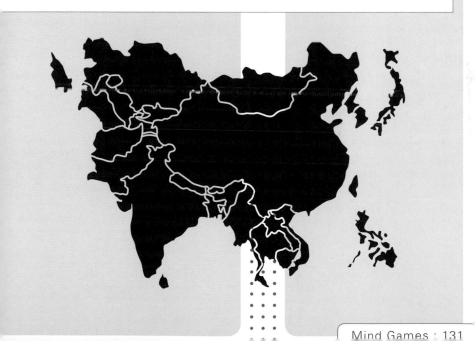

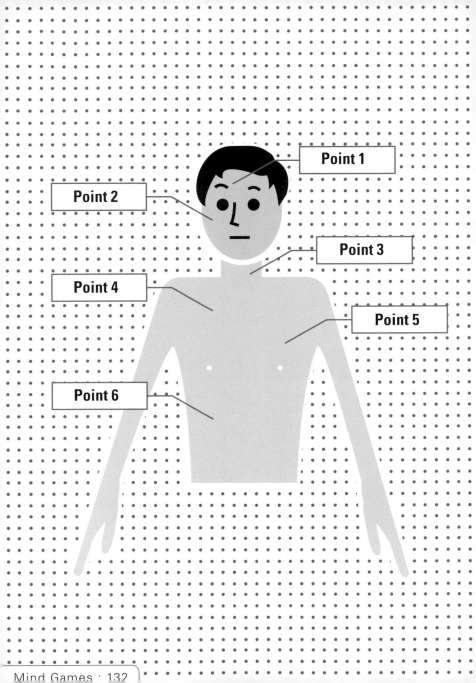

Point 1

Point 2

Point 3

Point 4

Point 5

Point 6

Simple Neck and Shoulder Self-Acupressure

The diagram shows the important acupoints in the upper torso. You can find them with your fingers by looking for areas that feel tender or tense when you apply gentle pressure. As you locate each point, squeeze or press with gentle firmness until you feel your body responding. Don't press so hard that you feel unbearable pain, but you may experience a "good" pain—one that you know signals a release of tension. Often pain comes after a tense muscle is allowed to relax.

Lie on the floor with a book underneath your head so that it is neither scrunched back or jammed forward but is in line with the rest of your spine. With your hands on your tummy, spend a moment breathing deeply into your hands, allowing your breath to reach deep into your abdomen rather than remain locked in your chest.

Then apply gentle but firm pressure to the muscles along the base of the skull using your thumbs, beginning with your ears and moving down towards the spine. Concentrate on those parts that feel tense or tender until they soften and release. You may already feel the blood flow increase along the back of your neck.

Now bring a hand across your chest and squeeze the neck and shoulders and repeat with the other hand on the other side. Continue to breathe deeply as you press and release.

Finally, return your hands to your abdomen and allow your head to feel heavy as you roll it gently from side to side and round in a gentle circle, first clockwise, then counterclockwise.

Spend about 10 minutes on this exercise; then when you are ready to stand up, slowly roll over onto your side, onto all fours, then gently arise. You may feel a bit light headed and a tingling sensation in your neck and shoulders—a sign that the blood supply to your brain has improved. Take a moment to come back to earth.

49

This is similar to speed reading (see page 56), only with this technique you can summarize an entire book in just 10 minutes. It is a great skill to use when you have a lot of research to complete and you need to gain an overview of each book before you begin closer study of a few key texts.

All you need is a timer, a pen, and several Post-It® notes or scraps of paper. Start the timer and open your book. Turn each page and scan very quickly. Each page should take seconds. Remember you've only got 10 minutes for the whole book, so if there are 200 pages that's just three seconds per page, so don't dawdle!

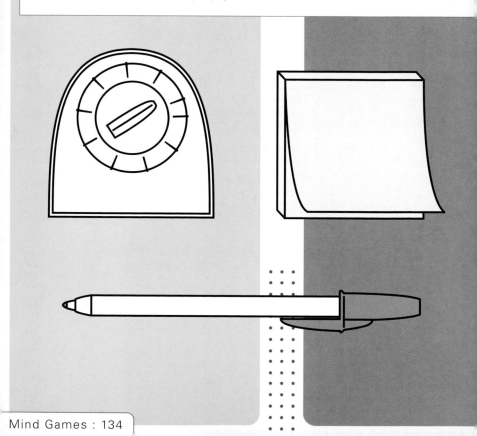

You're not trying to read the book. You want to gain an overview that will tell you:

1. How the book is arranged (sections, chapters)
2. Key themes and summary points
3. Areas of special interest/relevance

If something catches your attention, mark it with a scrap of paper or Post-It note so you can read it properly later. It is very important that you stick to the 10-minute time limit.

Afterwards spend no more than five minutes creating a brief visual summary of the book (called a Mind Map). Do it from memory and you'll be surprised how much information you have assimilated about the structure and content. Much of learning is knowing where to find information; the learning bit is the icing on the cake and a separate skill.

If you power browse all the books that you plan to use to research a topic before you begin in-depth reading, you will dramatically improve your concentration, since you will know the general areas you need to cover and where to find them.

You will already have gained a broad overview of the subject, since some themes and features will be repeated in many of the books, alerting you to the fact that they are the most important. You will also greatly reduce time spent flitting from one book to another. Some of the books you won't even have to read at all beyond the initial power browse because you know that similar topics have been covered elsewhere.

Power browsing is a powerful tool because it gives you a framework within which to operate. Context is an all-important part of the learning process.

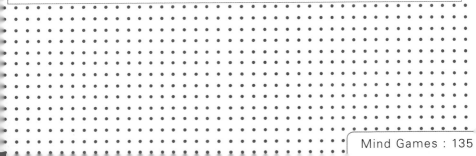

The problem with most stress-reduction programs is that they're just that—programs, lectures, courses, tapes, CDs, weekend retreats—involving hours of deep breathing, meditation, and New Age gimmicks. But they're just not "portable." Here are 10 simple, no nonsense ideas that are easy to remember, quick to perform, and a highly effective way to reboot your neurological system.

Slow Down

Take Five

When you feel the anxiety rising and your composure is beginning to slip, use a watch to consciously slow down your breathing to six breaths a minute (inhale for five seconds, exhale for five seconds) and keep it going until your anxiety reduces.

Take 60 Seconds

Sometimes even five minutes is a luxury. Spare a minute to close your eyes and breathe deeply and slowly. Imagine that you are walking in a sunny meadow or taking a refreshing shower in a waterfall.

Take a Vacation

Close your eyes, smile, and whisk yourself away to a real vacation destination that was special and relaxing. Try to remember the smells and sounds.

Yawn

This is one of the best ways to increase your oxygen intake and relax the tension that builds up in your jaw and face. If anyone raises an eyebrow, tell them it's a power yawn.

Shopping List

It can be mentally exhausting to keep a list of worries and concerns in your head. Instead, write them all down, put the list in your pocket, and wipe them from your memory. This will free up precious brain space and give you better concentration.

House payment
Does my wife love me?
My health
My job
Car broke down

Windmill

Speed Up

Body Yawn

Have you noticed how animals yawn with their entire bodies? They don't stifle it with their sleeve, they have a really good stretch and even a back rub. So go on—arch your back, flex your fingers, and make a loud yawning noise to shake the birds out of the trees. And if no one is watching, lie down and grind your back on the floor.

I-Pod Power

Put some zing back in your step with some lively music. Forget the Mozart and Brian Eno, we're talking cannons or a back beat. Jack your body and get psyched.

Slap and Tickle

Shake your hands loosely for 30 seconds then slap all over your body to wake you up and get the blood flowing. Rub your ears briskly and stretch your lobes. Tap your forehead and your cheeks, legs, arms, and chest until you feel warm and tingling all over.

Windmill

Stand up and with your arms straight out to the sides, so your body forms a "T" shape. Begin to draw tiny circles with your arms by rotating clockwise from the shoulders. Gradually make the circles bigger and bigger until you are drawing the biggest circles possible without doing yourself an injury, then shrink the circle again and come to rest.

Laugh

It's not always easy to find something to laugh about, but even a pretend laugh combined with a big fake smile and raised eyebrows will lift your mood and make you feel more energetic.

Index

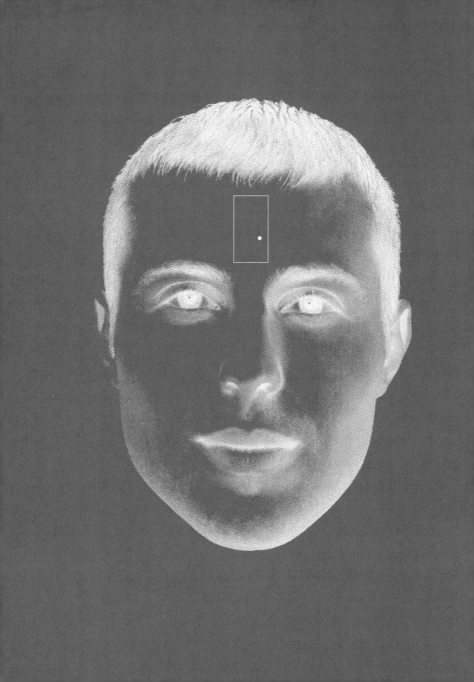